The Varmits: Living with Appalachian Outlaws

A Memoir

By

Ted Coonfield

For Frankie
a "Varmit"
at heart and
just a fun guy!
Enjoy these
stories.

Ted C.
"Scoop"

authorHOUSE®

AuthorHouse™
1663 Liberty Drive
Bloomington, IN 47403
www.authorhouse.com
Phone: 1-800-839-8640

First published by AuthorHouse   08/15/2011

ISBN: 978-1-4567-3354-4 (sc)
ISBN: 978-1-4567-3355-1 (hc)
ISBN: 978-1-4567-3353-7 (ebk)

Library of Congress Control Number 2011900916

Printed in the United States of America

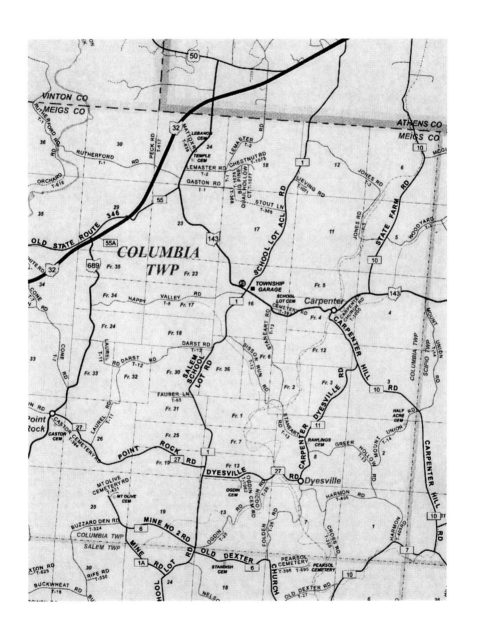

Dedication

To my friends and family, who mostly will not be surprised, but most of whom will still love me for what I became, thankfully.

In Memoriam

Joseph "Little Joe" Strassman, 1950-2008

Michael "Mini" Radebaugh, 1954-1993

David "Hip" Hunt, 1951-2011

The Varmits: Living with Appalachian Outlaws

Prologue

Varmint, n. **1.** *Chiefly Southern, and South Midland U.S.* **a.** vermin. **b.** an objectionable or undesirable animal, usually predatory, as a coyote or bobcat. **2.** A despicable, obnoxious, or annoying person. Also **var'ment** (1530-40, var. of vermin.)
Webster's Unabridged Dictionary, Second Edition. Random House, New York, 1998.

Varmit, n. **1.** *Chiefly Southeast Ohio U.S.* Name of non-conforming self-chosen outcasts who lived in Meigs County, Ohio, grew marijuana, raised fighting cocks, screwed women, listened to the Grateful Dead, drank beer, and played softball (1970s). **2.** See number 2 above.

Smack dab in the middle of Appalachia and the seventies, I lived on a thirty-acre farm about sixteen miles from Athens, Ohio, with a dog, two cats, some geese, turkeys, chickens, a pond, and a root cellar. This plot of land would be my teacher, my home, and my love, and it was surrounded by "Varmits." Whether the misspelling was deliberate or inadvertent is unclear, but it didn't matter, that's for sure. These young men and their ladies had left the outside world behind, the one they did not really trust. To the extent that the outside world knew them at all, they were perceived as misguided and misbegotten miscreants, and perhaps they were. But I soon found out they were so much more. The Varmits' informal community evolved over a few years in the early seventies, living in the hills and hollers of the rolling terrain of Meigs County, for free or low rent in neglected farm houses, decrepit barns, ancient log cabins, and rickety trailers.

Although clichéd, this is a story about sex, drugs, and rock 'n' roll. It is a story about a softball team, a cock fight, pornography, a barn full of marijuana, skinny-dipping, and friendship. But it is also a story about scholarship, research, famous people, taking Ph.D. comprehensives, creating organizations, leading one, and preparing for life in the corporate world.

It is a story about learning the law of the country, taking care of animals, growing a garden, killing chickens, roasting a pig, remodeling a house, skimming cream, making butter, fixing a water pump, canning fresh produce, growing magic mushrooms, and talking to a giant tree who became my friend.

This is a story about contrasting worlds: one in a quaint university town, one in the country; one in academia, one in Appalachia; one with scholars, one with derelicts; one with traditional Christian friends, one with porn-watching school pals; one involving advising a University President, one about advising the Varmits how to run a softball tournament; one requiring giving a speech to thousands; one about sitting alone peacefully in the country watching fireflies flicker in the night.

Ultimately, this is a story about a young man in his twenties shedding much of the yoke of his heritage and transitioning from a middle-class Southern gentleman upbringing, albeit sexist, in the 1950s and 1960s, into a man who could relate to women more equally by understanding them as powerful and varied human beings.

The Varmits took care of their own. They shared food and money, bailed their comrades out of jail, built barns together, fixed each others' trucks, harvested fields cooperatively, and generally created a wild and loose but loving community amidst the hills of Southeast Ohio. They even ex-communicated one of their own who lied and cheated in a drug deal. He was banished from association with the group and barred from ever calling himself a Varmit again. But after years of either forgiveness or forgetfulness, they reinstated him for the Reunion in 2004. As Bob the Varmit told me one time when I asked him about some of the group's more nefarious activities, "Scoop, we weren't crooks, just outlaws." This is my story of how I became a Varmit—or at least a good bit of one—and how I became damn proud of it.

Author's Notes

When the events of this story were unfolding, I kept no diary and wrote no notes. No thought of ever writing a book about the experience possessed me. So now I approach the literary genre they call "memoir." This story is as true as I can make it. But you, the reader, should realize that my memory is clouded by a historical haze of dope and mushrooms, the distractions of life, and the passage of more than three decades. The mind can be a bizarre fabricator and dreams can invade and obfuscate—all that is at work here. For example, when I visited with Fred, my turkey buddy whom I had not seen in thirty years, he told me that he had helped butcher the pig. I had some vague recollection of that, so I wrote it that way. In another instance, when the book was nearly done, Varmit Bob explained to me that I had totally messed up the fact that the Baron's softball team never did play in that first softball tournament, that they actually played in the one we sponsored a year later. I love that chapter, and decided to leave it alone. So it is just plain inaccurate. Did Abby actually give me Germaine Greer's book? I don't really recall, but we talked about it and she certainly led me to it.

The events took place beginning in the summer of 1974, through fall, winter, spring, and the next summer of 1975. I tried to be true to the approximate time within those seasons.

Dr. Jimmy Corder, my major professor at Texas Christian University, wrote a memoir called *Chronicles of a Small Town*. He struggled to reconcile his childhood memories with old copies of his little Texas town newspaper from the 1930s and 1940s. The surprises, mental mishaps, contradictory data, and conundrums of comparing one's memory with journalism somewhat overwhelmed him. He wrote: "I've tried to understand what there is about my thinking that would cause or lead me to remember some things but not others and to remember some things wrong, but I have only partial explanations." I feel the same way.

Some names have been changed to protect the good and the guilty, but most names are real. I actually only give one last name away of those living, but it is a public record anyway. Dear friends who adorn these pages: please forgive me if I describe you not as you would have it. It is only my perspective. Most everyone written about here is better, smarter, and lovelier than he or she was then, that's a fact. Dear friends whom I have left out: it was only for literary requirements or convenience or faulty memory, not for lack of respect or love that you did not make it into these pages.

With respect to those who have known me in other contexts, relatives, friends of relatives, classmates, teachers, work colleagues and professional associates: it is not my intent to offend, shock, or otherwise shade your perceptions of me or my values. Even given the transgressions and derelictions of youth, all of my experiences have only contributed to, never shattered or deeply disturbed, the core values I learned in early years from parents, schools, church, and community activities. As much as this book is part of me, it is not all of me.

To my young friends and relatives, please understand that I had two years of college behind me before I ever drank alcohol; and a master's degree before I ever smoked dope or consumed magic mushrooms. I never took any drugs except those prescribed by a physician, well, except for the few times I experimented with the effects of snorting cocaine in my thirties. I am not advocating for drug use, only accounting experiences from another time and place, with the full awareness that youth and drugs can be an unhealthy or even fatal combination.

To the universities involved in my life, please do not be offended by the cynicism of youth represented here. Both universities served me magnificently, and are wonderful institutions of higher education. I am proud to have been associated with both of them.

This book had to wait until my parents died, for it would have only proved their suspicions, and until I retired, so no prospective employer who searched the internet for information about me would have a ready excuse not to hire me.

All of us have stories to tell. Those involved in this one could surely embellish and expand upon what I describe. They certainly lived it, and all see it differently than I. So be gentle with me, dear friends and readers. Please don't scold me for my montage of memory, as accurate and fallible as it is. Write your own stories down, post them on the website or in a blog, or write your own damn book.

I can accept responsibility for errors of fact, but each of us has our personal perspectives, recollections, and memories, and, as in religion and taste in wine, each of us is our own final authority.

Ted Coonfield
2011

Maybe Imagination is just
a form of memory after all, locked
deep in the double helix of eternity.
Or maybe the past is but one more
phantasmagoric invention we use
to fool ourselves into someone else's shoes.
    (Ronald Wallace, "Off the Record")

Chapter 1: Moving to the Country

Sometimes we live no
particular way but our own
Sometimes we visit your country
and live in your home
      (Robert Hunter and Jerry Garcia, "Eyes of the World")

WANTED—RESPONSIBLE COUPLE to rent secluded farm house-30 acres, farm, pond, bath, fireplace, furniture, must rent for 1 yr. available June 1 $125/mo. 698-2626, 698-4375.

    Living in the country possessed me. An oddity, given the fact I grew up in suburban Oklahoma City, just six blocks off the highway of the Heartland, Route 66. The neighborhood was filled with similar houses of different color brick, all ranch-style three-bedroom homes with two-car garages, chain-link fenced back yards, barbeque grills on cement patios, and home milk delivery. We played baseball in the daytime and kick-the-can in the evenings. My friends and I toilet-papered the houses of cute girls, and became sticky and hairy pugilists in rotten tomato and cattail fights at the local "lake": a gravel pit abandoned by a concrete company and filled with water and snakes, copperheads to be exact. It was an urban existence with just a little bit of the country, and now I wanted more than a taste. I was ready to immerse myself in all things rural. So I was excited to be heading out of Athens, Ohio, on Highway 50, past Albany and down County Road C-10 through a ghost town called Carpenter, with one old abandoned and deteriorating general store, a Baptist church, and a handful of houses hugging the hills, and with the Leading Creek and railroad tracks both dissecting the ghost town. Climbing the curved hill "out of town" I noticed the biggest tree I think I'd ever seen. Months later I learned the tree's species, a Catawba, with giant leaves, and a wingspan covering what seemed like a city block, or whatever they call "a shitload of land" in the country. It would become my friend over the next two years, and talking to the tree as I drove by didn't seem so strange in a county where I was soon to discover that strangeness was the accepted norm, and where "characters" dwelt on every hill, and in every holler, and down every lane.

I answered an ad in the Ohio University newspaper about a 30-acre farm for rent, and being possessed to live in the country, I thought it destiny. It was spring of 1974, and with the first year of my doctoral studies in communication almost behind me, I desperately wanted to leave my single dorm room on the South Green behind. I could touch both walls of that room when putting on a shirt, and I had come to realize that a single bed in a small room not only limited dressing and sleeping, it imposed severe romantic restraint.

"Hello, is this the country place advertised for rent?" I asked on the phone.

"Well, no, this is Mickey," the voice wisecracked, "but I got a place here I'm renting."

"Is it still available?"

"Yea, but we have had a lot of calls and I've already done a few interviews, so it's now or never."

"How long does it take to get there from Athens?"

"Oh, only about 20-25 minutes," Mickey estimated.

"I'll be there in 30; please don't rent it before then," I pleaded.

"OK, we can probably wait that long," Mickey chuckled.

I left the pavement behind just outside Carpenter following the gravel road up the hill past a large sheep farm and cresting at the Dyesville road intersection. I steered my old maroon Impala down a long winding hill to the valley floor, dotted with a couple of trailers and a very old log cabin on the right. The entryway to the property was just as Mickey described: "Follow the gravel drive with the grassy knoll in the middle to the partially graveled parking lot by the creek, cross the bridge, walk up the road, past the chicken coop and goose pen, and we'll be in the house. They call this Copperhead Hollow, you know. You drink coffee?"

"No thanks, but I love hot tea," I replied.

"We'll put a kettle on for you."

Copperhead Hollow, I thought. How did those snakes migrate all the way back east from Oklahoma?

The "we" turned out to be Mickey and his wife, Anise. Transplanted Easterners, I guessed. Their accents and trappings of ethnicity gave them away. It was mutual interest at first sight, interesting for an Okie, who had only months before discovered that bagels were not just hard, inedible donuts; interesting for Mickey and Anise, who had visions of Native Americans living in teepees way out there on the prairie.

Offered tea, I sat in the small, slate-floored and old lath-paneled living room with its big stone fire place taking up most of one wall. Mickey said, "I didn't get your last name on the phone."

"It's Coonfield, spelled C-O-O-N-F-I-E-L-D, just like it sounds. I got the name from my parents."

They both just cracked up with laughter, not at my attempt at humor, but because of a coincidence they found irresistibly funny. Anise yelled out, "Cranfield, come! Cranfield, come on in here boy!" I heard the door bang shut and in bounded a large German shepherd, who immediately trotted over to sniff me a good one. I patted him on the head, not a small gesture for one who has been terrified of and allergic to dogs most of his entire life. Well, you can fool some of the dogs some of the time. Cranfield looked past my shortcomings and curled up around my feet with obvious satisfaction. Mickey and Anise looked on like satisfied Yentas having just consummated a successful union.

"Maybe Cranfield and I will be the couple you wanted," I offered, trying to make light of the fact that I obviously was not a couple as the ad had specified. I feared that they might be hesitant to rent to a single guy in his twenties, a demographic hardly trustworthy with your home, not to mention your daughter, and other things.

"You said you were a student at OU, What are you studying?" Mickey asked. (Even after a year in Ohio, this Okie had trouble not thinking "boomer, sooner" whenever he heard "OU")

"I'm doing a Ph.D. in the School of Interpersonal Communication. You know, the old speech department, with debate, group dynamics, public-speaking, interpersonal, intercultural, and organizational communication, and rhetorical studies."

Mickey sat still with a puzzled look, obviously processing all those words very carefully. After a deliberate moment, Mickey deadpanned, "Jeez, I didn't realize that university gave degrees in hodgepodge." I may have laughed, but more likely I just changed the subject.

"How long will you be gone on the trip you mentioned on the phone?" I inquired. Anise responded that they wanted to take at least a year, driving through Central America and visiting every South American country. "Ambitious," I thought. I was even more surprised when Mickey proudly stated they were going to do it in the old Volvo sports car parked out front. As if hearing my silent concern, Mickey explained, "I got a box in the back with enough parts to totally rebuild the engine if we need to."

Having no inkling about the mechanics of cars, I was duly impressed.

We chatted for a good while about taking care of the place and the animals. I waxed eloquently about my father growing up a farmer and coming from hardy Okie stock. I declared I wanted to plant a garden, eat a lot of peaches, can some tomatoes, let others find Jesus, and enjoy the solitude of the country to study and write. Of course, my actual days in the country to that point in life were numbered on one hand, and they were always punctuated by allergic attacks. But what the hell, living in the country possessed me, and I was meant to be there. Never shying away from a passionate appeal, I told them how much I wanted to live in the country, how I always left a place better than I had found it, and how I loved animals and wanted to experiment with self-sufficiency. It was a load of mostly bullshit, but hey, when you're possessed, you cannot be totally responsible for your own behavior. Anyway, Mickey said he'd call and let me know one way or the other, for they still had some more interviews to do.

Prayer in my life had mostly waned, but if there was any facsimile of cosmic justice left in the world, the place should be mine. Two days later, I got the call. Mickey and Anise just couldn't get over the Coonfield/Cranfield coincidence, so they were ready to rent their little farm to me. I had encountered a couple who had morphed from Brooklyn suffer-no-fools-realists into way-kum-ba-ya hippies, and the balance of cosmic justice had tilted in my favor. I was moving to the country. Somehow they overlooked the "couple" thing, or maybe they bought my line about Cranfield and me being a couple. Anyway, I could cook and clean with the best of the female clan, and what the heck, Cranfield could lick the plates. Lyrics sang in my head.

> Gonna leave the city put my troubles behind
> People in the city goin' out of their minds
> Goin' to the country just to feel like gold
> People in the country really let themselves go
>
> Goin' to the country and leavin' right away
> No time to talk, I got to make a getaway
> Gonna leave the city, it's a crime and a shame
> People in the city are goin' insane.
> (Steve Miller and Ben Sidran, "Going To the Country")

I called my parents and told them I got the place and would move in a few weeks, after spring quarter classes were over. My father, not really wanting to rain on my parade, but oozing vibes I could feel over the phone, said simply, "That's interesting. Can you afford the rent?" How could such a seemingly caring and innocuous question imply to me so many other things like, "Do you have any idea what you're doing, what responsibilities you're incurring, how little you know about animals, gardening, and fixing equipment? What about the commute, will your studies suffer, and who's going to be your roommate?" Yep, I heard those things, yet all unspoken by the Major.

"Yes, I can afford the rent 'cause I plan to split it with a roommate," I comforted. "Anyway, it's what I want to do, and I can learn how to do a lot of cool things, like gardening and canning."

That logic my parents understood. They had a long history of knowing I was going to do what I wanted to do, and the realities of life were not as important as getting what I wanted. Spoiled? No, let's call it determined.

In mid-May, the oaks were in full leaf, the grass green, the air clean, the sun bright, and the country calling. I was moving to Meigs County, Ohio, home to one of the largest deep coal mines in the world at the time, with a conveyor belt stretching across the rolling hills to a processing plant twenty-six miles away. What is Meigs, County, Ohio? It is the question that fits the Jeopardy answer "the poorest county in the state of Ohio." Lying in the foothills of Appalachia, the county is named for Return J. Meigs, Jr., the fourth Governor of Ohio. It's a mere 43 square miles of beautiful vistas and rolling forests, yet full of poverty, coal miners, farmers, moon shiners, and as I would soon learn, Varmits. It so happened that one of my college roommates, Greg, just out of a three-year gig as an officer in the Marine Corps, wanted to come to OU to do a master's degree in economics and could room with me that first summer. The stars were aligned, but not for long.

Moving in was a piece of cake. I was going from a tiny dorm room cell to a furnished country place and most everything fit in the old Impala my father had bestowed upon me. With a secondhand mattress and box spring tied across the roof, I retraced my route from Athens to Meigs County with new excitement and countrified eagerness. Out of Carpenter, I again did a double take by the big old Catawba tree and said spontaneously, "Old tree, I'm goin' be your neighbor, and I bet you got some stories to tell."

The wind nodded the biggest of the swooping branches and the tree seemed to reply, "You're so right my boy. There are lots of stories in these hills, and some are mostly true."

It had rained earlier in the day so the road from the parking lot to the house was quite muddy and draining the last of the runoff. "I need to buy some rubber overshoes," I thought as I sloshed ahead up the hill. The entrance to the house was through both a ratty torn screen and old wood panel door into a small kitchen with a sink and an old-fashioned water pump (yep, no hot running water in that room), a large, red, square oil heater, a fridge, and a few haphazardly strewn cabinets tacked around the edges to the wall. The kitchen opened into the dining room with a big oak table in the middle surrounded by antique rickety pressed-back oak chairs, a giant pot-bellied heating stove with nickel-plated ornamentation adorning the base and top, which now, in reflection, reminds me of the grill of my 1954 Chevy pickup truck. Narrow, rough-hewn floor to ceiling shelves covered one wall. They would become perfect for storing and displaying all the canned goods from the garden. Occupying corners were a few quintessentially seventies plants: wandering Jew, avocado, fern, and something so weird-looking I did not recognize it, but it was definitive evidence that maybe plants did absorb dope smoke after all. A double French door opened into the small living room with its massive rock fireplace, slate flooring (recycled from the farmhouse roof), and swayback, threadbare, pinkish couch next to a lamp and end table. Right in the middle of these three rooms was a steep and narrow set of stairs that led to the attic. It was un-insulated, and hardly high enough for my tallish frame, but it would become my bedroom. Summer, fall, winter, and spring, whatever the weather was outdoors, it was exactly the same up those stairs. Next to the stairs, a hallway led to the bath with sink, tub, toilet, and window. The walls were covered with burlap, which, unfortunately, absorbed all the odors produced within those walls. Our only hot water sprang forth from the tub and sink spigots. Past the bath, the hall ended in a little corner bedroom with space enough for a single bed and small desk. "Toto, we're a long way from suburbia," I thought to myself.

I had the first week to myself before Greg arrived from his spit-and-polish days as a jarhead. And I had just learned that another college friend was coming for a visit as well. Everything seemed to be going along quite well: Cranfield and I were buddies, and he introduced me to the other members of the animal menagerie vested in my care. They included one tiger-striped cat with three legs named Rutabaga, and a pure white cat with one green eye and one blue eye, deafer than a door knob and named Succubus, some famous mythical character that the lusty Anise thought cool. Being a curious scholar, I looked the name up in the dictionary, and lo and behold Succubus was a "demon in female form, said to have sexual intercourse with men in their sleep."

"I must remember to shut the door to the attic at night," I thought. It did add quite a new twist to getting some pussy, and the sexual cat thing would come back later to haunt me, but that's another story. I learned to not underestimate cats with disabilities, for Rutabaga was as fast on three legs as the fastest four-legged fur ball, and Succubus could see, feel, touch, and smell far better than her hearing counterparts. They were ferocious hunters of rats and other rodents in Copperhead Hollow, but in the evening they would curl up on my lap (or that of any willing visitor), snuggle in for a long winter's nap, and become soft and sensual purring machines. I would not let Succubus too close to my naughty bits (as the English say) for quite some time, until we developed a mutual understanding of what each of us meant by the words pussy and sex.

The tranquility of the country was growing on me, although I confess that I was feeling the need for more social action. Daily chores fit in between the commute to class, for the chickens, geese, the dog, and cats needed their daily feeding and watering.

One day, walking the road in my newly purchased rubber slippers an eerie feeling welled in my gut as I crested the rise and stepped onto the lawn leading to the house. Something was just not right. Something was different, and it spooked me. The door had been jimmied and broken loose, and with trepidation I stepped inside. Clearly the invaders had violated the tranquility of my space. A quick reconnaissance of the place revealed that no one was there; I breathed a sigh of relief. But I'd been ripped off. My little dorm room stereo was gone, with turntable, speakers, and all. All the cabinets had been rifled through, the chest-of-drawers ransacked. The pitted stomach knot nauseated my innards. "Welcome to the country," I thought sarcastically. A few moments of reflection brought me to realize little harm had been done: the door was repairable, the stereo easily replaceable, and the clean-up would only take an hour or so of angry distraction.

That evening, sitting alone at the big ol' oak table, still a little depressed about being violated, I thought about conflict and communication, the country and community, common interest and criminal behavior. I hit upon the idea that maybe the neighbors would have seen or known of something that day, so I vowed to go do some investigating with a little reverse Welcome Wagon strategy and introduce myself to the neighbors. That's when I met the Varmits.

Chapter 2: Irv and Little Joe Indoctrination

I wasn't raised to rip off friends, I'm low, not out the bottom.
Odd beginnings have common ends, ask the ones who brought 'em.
    (Robert Hunter, "Ithica")

The nearest place was a venerable log cabin across the road and up the hill, good enough as any place to start my sleuthing and ol' timey meetin' and greetin'. Old farm equipment sat rusting in the front and on the sides of the cabin; no one seemed to be around except a swayback horse and a very old donkey. Dick the Donkey, to be exact, I soon learned. With no inkling of what I might encounter, I boldly knocked on the rickety door.

"Who's there?" a voice called back.

"I'm your new neighbor across the road," I replied.

The door opened and there stood a man, I guessed thirtyish, in jeans hanging below his narrow hip bones, and no shirt, revealing the sculptured body of an athlete, but not a recent one. His long, blondish beard pointed sharply at his navel, and his long hair was tied back in a pony-tail, not the look of a current college athlete.

"Where did you say you lived?" he asked.

"Across the street, ah, road, at Mickey and Anise's place. My name is Ted." I stuck out my hand.

With a slightly wry grin, he shook my hand and said, "Mine's Irv." As I recounted my recent episode of robbery in the country, Irv listened rather attentively, and with some sympathy said he didn't know of any banditos in the neighborhood, had heard nothing, and was sorry for my hassle. As he was talking, I glanced behind him at movement in the cabin and saw a naked girl walk by the door in a little room in the back. Refrains of Paul Simon's "Cecelia" hummed in my head, *making love in the afternoon with Cecelia up in my bedroom . . .*

Irv suggested I check with a Little Joe who lived down the road. Irv indicated that Joe would know all without admitting any guilt or knowledge, a rare skill of interpersonal and psychological prowess I would later learn that Little Joe had honed to a fine art. Not wanting to just focus on my mission of investigation, I asked, "Did you build this cabin?"

"No" Irv replied, "It's over 150 years old, one of the oldest in the county."

"What do you do?" I continued my neighborly questioning.

"Well, pretty much anything I want. But who a man is, now that's more important than what he does, like for a living."

"Wow, a regular, local philosopher," I thought. But that was the last time I ever asked a Varmit what he did, for it was never important to them to talk of occupations and jobs. They left that behind in another world and time, and besides, how could one respond truthfully when dope-growing, drug-selling, cock-fighting and other nefarious income streams might be the case?

"Where does this Little Joe live?" I asked.

"Down the hill just past your driveway on the right, kinda offset from the road in the river bottom land." Irv pointed off to his right.

"Thanks," I toned, heading off in investigative zeal. What the log cabin was to 150 years of neglect, Little Joe's house made up for it with only thirty or forty years of benign non-effort. Dogs, cats, ice boxes, cars, farm equipment, and old carpet decorated the yard of a newer but ratty frame farmhouse with peeling paint, a precarious porch missing deck boards, and a screen door that banged and clattered when left to slam. I wasn't even out of the car when I heard rock standards of the Grateful Dead blaring out through the broken windows and screen door. Glancing out past the house, I saw fields partly planted near a stream, with a forest rising on the hill behind. Again, not quite knowing what to expect, I knocked on the door while eyeing a mangy old dog for fear he would rise up to protect the household, my mind trying not to believe the old adage that the houses of thieves are always protected by vicious attack dogs. But the dog stayed still and silent and so did the house. It must take more to penetrate the beat of the Dead, so my knocking became banging and it was only the rattling of the rafters and shaking of the walls that I thought stirred anyone.

From nowhere it seemed, but actually around the corner of the house, came a little guy dressed in a dirty white T-shirt, ragged jeans, and bare feet. "Whatcha want, man?" he asked.

Now knowing one local, I replied, "Irv up the road sent me to check with a Little Joe. Are you him?"

Now that was a truly stupid question, for before me stood a young man who was a mutant cross between a regular guy in his twenties and a hobbit, a little person that grew up slightly or a regular guy who didn't. I reached out to offer a handshake and as he approached to reciprocate, it hit me. This munchkin reeked of dope smoke, and I mean not subtly.

"Yea, that's what they call me," he droned with an oh-so-slight hint of Brooklyn in his speech. I recounted my conversation with Irv, the dastardly deed of being ripped off, and where I lived across the road. He said he didn't know anything about it, but his quick denial left me with one of those feelings of unknown origins that he knew more than he revealed. I might want to put one Little Joe on my suspect list. It was during this mental machination that I caught out of the corner of my eye a human figure in the doorway.

"What's happening?" I said. He nodded. Little Joe said that was Tweeter, a friend visiting from California. We chit-chatted a little while, and then he paused, kinda eye-balling my six foot three inch, 185-pound frame before asking, "Do you play softball?"

"I used to play church softball, and lots of baseball as a kid and in high school. Why you ask?"

"We got a pick-up game over at the Dust Bowl this Sunday, and we're always looking for players. Since you live out here on the Ridge with us now, we could consider you a new prospect for our team."

Priding myself on athletic prowess, particularly in comparison to this tiny troll, and loving to play ball games of all kinds, I quickly thought that a little local get together to play a couple of games of softball would be innocent enough and fun. At least the fun part turned out to be true.

26

It was then, maybe to bond with a new recruit, that Little Joe pulled out a pretty good size joint, lit it up, and offered me a toke. There was no pomp and circumstance to the gesture, for he made it look as natural as a member of the English gentry pouring someone a cup of tea. I said, "Thanks," and took a long drag on the bigger-than-a-cigarette-sized joint. By the time we got to roach-clip size, I was pretty wasted. Who knew what we talked about or what music was playing, but I did notice a young woman who entered the room with a little baby straddling her oh-so-small hips. In fact, upon focusing nonchalantly, I could see her body was so diminutive that she looked like a twelve-year-old holding her little newborn sister. Of course, she wasn't, and little Joe introduced her saying, "This is Valerie and her baby Stephanie. They're crashing here for a while," and leaving it at that.

I said my thanks and good-byes and in my Okie hospitality mode offered our pond anytime they wanted to come up for dip. I drifted back across the gravel road, crossed the little bridge, and headed up the drive to the house. It was then with geese honking, Cranfield running up for a pet, and a deep satisfaction that comes with good Meigs County weed overtaking me, that I named the place in my somewhat altered head, creative as it may seem, The Country Place.

I would get to know lots of other characters in the next few months. One day, a little bored of studying models of communication at the university library, I wandered over to the reference desk to inquire how to learn about historical characters from Meigs County. The reference librarian directed me to an anthology and in a matter of minutes I learned that not a lot of famous people had been born or lived in Meigs County. The exception, one of its few favorite sons, Ambrose Gwinnett Bierce, was born near Horse Cave Creek in 1842. There is a plaque about him in front of Eastern High School in Chester. This guy definitely had Meigs County in his blood. Known as an American journalist, editorialist, short story writer, satirist, and fabulist, he is best remembered for his famous short story "An Occurrence at Owl Creek Bridge" and his satirical lexicon *The Devil's Dictionary.* As a vicious critic, he earned the nickname "Bitter Bierce." He served as a First Lieutenant in the Union Army during the Civil War, fighting in the Battle of Shiloh, and subsequently penned a memoir entitled "What I Saw at Shiloh." After the Civil War, he inspected outposts throughout the West and ended up in San Francisco. Bierce married Mary Ellen "Mollie" Day on Christmas day, 1871. They had three children, a daughter and two sons. Bierce's sons died before him, one of pneumonia related to alcoholism and the other was shot in a brawl over a woman. Bierce separated from his wife in 1888 after discovering compromising letters to her from an admirer, and the couple finally divorced in 1904. Mollie Day Bierce died the following year. Bierce suffered from lifelong asthma as well as complications arising from his war wounds. Curious about the revolution in Mexico, he traveled there and while imbedded with Pancho Villa and his rebel troops, disappeared around 1914.

I found a copy of his *Devil's Dictionary* in a dusty stack in the far reaches of the library. It is absurd, erudite, irreverent, witty, sardonic, thought-provoking, and not an easy read. He basically makes up his own definitions for words. For example:

> Senate, n. A body of elderly gentlemen charged with high duties and misdemeanors.

> Self-esteem, n. An erroneous appraisement.

> Self-evident, adj. Evident to one's self and nobody else.

> Corporation, n. An ingenious device for obtaining individual profit without individual responsibility.

> Age, n. That period of life in which we compound for the vices that we still cherish by reviling those that we have no longer the enterprise to commit.

> Story, n. A narrative, commonly untrue. The truth of stories here following has, however, not been successfully impeached.

I noted in my research that Meigs County was founded on April Fool's Day, 1819. Was I a fool for moving there? Would I meet fools already living there? I thought to myself while leaving the library for Meigs County, while a renewed curiosity reverberated in my head.

Chapter 3: Summer School
and Schools of Fish

If this were love now how would I know? How would I know?
Feel like a stranger
Gonna be a long, long, crazy, crazy night
Silky, silky, crazy, crazy night
      (John Barlow and Bob Weir, "Feel Like a Stranger")

The next day I drove to Athens to begin summer school at Ohio University, the "Harvard on the Hocking" as the T-shirts hanging in the store windows of Court Street proudly proclaimed. By now I was a veteran of a Ph.D. program, having survived the first year of tough courses as a scared newbie, acting as a teaching assistant for an absentee professor, teaching an undergraduate course in Interpersonal Communication, and remaining ambulatory and taking sustenance in spite of existing in a South Green dorm room where, like I said, when I put on a shirt with outstretched arms, my finger-tips touched both walls. It wasn't a cell, but close. Anyway, it was no place to hustle chicks, with neighbors, a single bed, and all the romantic ambiance of a conjugal visit in a prison.

Summer school was different. One particular morning I awakened very early upstairs at the farmhouse, birds chirping away, the warm sun already starting to heat the un-insulated attic room. I had a brief conversation with Cranfield, fed and watered him and the cats, threw some grain over the fence for the geese, smelled the myriad aromas of the country air, and thought to myself, "Now this is living."

The drive across the rolling hills of Meigs County, dropping down onto Richland Avenue into Athens, just seemed liberating from the drudge walk up the hill from the South Green prison. Anyway, like I said, summer school was different. Let us not take school or ourselves too seriously in the good ol' summertime. Only, of course, to see the cycle beginning again in the fall when leaves turn and when professors pass out course syllabi, grade papers and administer tests, and actually do all the stuff that is blissfully neglected by deans, profs, and students alike in summer school. Early morning classes are actually motivating in summer, unlike in the dark, dead of winter. One can more easily get up in the light, and with classes and library work over by 2:00 PM, one can find lots of time to actually enjoy some leisurely pursuits other than being a scholar.

So across the College Green I bounced, leaving the library behind, and headed back to Kantner Hall which housed the School of Interpersonal Communication, the department which held my hopes for a degree in "hodgepodge." I never made it. The Baker Center, typical of the large student union buildings so central to residential American campuses, intercepted me with its patio overlooking the sidewalk, so perfect for lady-watching and beer-drinking.

Beckoned by a few male classmates to their table on the open deck, I ordered up a pitcher, we badmouthed the profs, discussed admiringly the anatomy of many passing-by coeds, and convinced ourselves that life does not get any better. With "homework" in the bag and no responsibilities in the country right away, I tipped my chair back and, for the first time since arriving in Athens, really felt like I was here as a person, not just a visiting student. Beer-drinking was the students of OU's destiny. The survey crew sent out to plot the original campus in 1787 had instructions to center the campus in what is now known as The Plains, a flat swath of land a few miles from Athens. The crew got drunk, lost their bearings, and surveyed one of the hilliest locales in the county. As it turned out, the campus occupies a beautiful location on the Hocking River, with the surrounding hills giving plenty of exercise to the student population and challenges to the architects and builders.

"Could you help me?" a female voice below on the sidewalk implored, arousing me from my near-nirvana slumber. Always willing to rescue a damsel in distress, I looked up from my very deep sense of satisfaction and there, with bike leaning on her hip, stood a young woman with a bike chain in her grease-covered hand and a look of slight desperation on her face. Now being a caring, sorta-kinda Christian type, my only call was to assist in her time of need. I failed to take note of her long legs and tight ass only so slightly covered by the über-skimpy and tight jean shorts. I hardly noticed that her halter-top was not doing a very good job of concealing her perky breasts, as if that was ever the intended purpose of the garment anyway.

"What seems to be the problem with the bike?" I asked in my best Good Samaritan voice.

"The chain came off, and I am clueless to figure out how to get this damn thing back on," she responded with appropriate disgust.

"Let me see what I can do," I said, heading to the end of the patio and down the steps on a mission to aid a stranded traveler. It did not take me too long to diagnose that her greasy chain was beyond function, and I calmly suggested that she get the bike to the shop before it closed if she really needed to use the bike anytime soon.

"The only bike shop I know is pretty far," she intoned.

Always one to go the extra mile to help someone in need, I told her I was heading that way out of town to my place in the country (a newfound pride of ownership and reality in my voice), and if she wanted, she could just throw her bike in the trunk of my car and I could drop her off there.

"Wow, that would be cool."

I picked up her bike, hoisted it to my shoulder in a manly fashion, and walked the couple of blocks down Union Street to my car. Never before had I so appreciated the massive trunk of a full-sized GM car.

"My name's Tracy, and I really appreciate your help," she volunteered.

"I'm Ted, and it's no problem."

As it turned out, the bike shop needed to keep the bike for a couple of days awaiting a part, so I asked Tracy where she needed to go and volunteered to drop her off there.

"Oh, I live in a little apartment over an aquarium on the other side of campus. Man, if you could drop me off that would be groovy, and I can always walk to school from there for a couple of days."

We wound through a near campus neighborhood of frame houses and fairly neat lawns. Interspersed were the not-so-neat student rental houses with old couches on the porches, beer cans scattered around the yards, peeling paint, and music escaping from the open doors and windows. Sure enough, she lived above a little aquarium store nestled right in the middle of this quaint little neighborhood.

"Just park there in the driveway; the shop is closed," she instructed. Awkwardly pausing before getting out of the car, Tracy looked over at me like she either had forgotten something or had a brainstorm and said, "Hey, I just got some good dope and as thanks could roll us up a joint if that interests you."

"What the hell?" I thought. It was summer, school was not until tomorrow, my summer roommates had not arrived, and Tracy was hot.

"Sure, that works for me," I coolly replied.

She offered me a seat on an old couch covered with a classic spread from India that smelled of yak, or at least what I thought yak should smell like. She dragged out a small tray and a little bag of pot and rolled us up a reefer. We smoked for a while and she said she got the stuff from a friend traveling through from California and it was called "California Sensimilla."

"Wow, killer pot," I breathed out in smoke.

"You want to check out something really far out?" she asked. "The shop up front is cool; let me show it to you."

It was almost dark as we entered the small business located in what was once the little living room of the frame house. She went over to a switch and, bingo, we were immersed in psychedelic wonder. The black lights that provide the showy medium for exotic tropical fish from all over the world splashed colors of Peter Max-like intensity around the room. Of course, we were fucked up and loving every sliver of dramatic light. Tracy went into a little back office, acquired a bottle of Cold Duck, popped the cork, and poured us a drink in some paper cups. She flipped another switch on the shelf, and the Doobie Brothers begin sending notes of music to intermingle with totally exotic Day-Glo fish swimming in an endless stream of tanks.

There was no place to flop in the middle of the aquarium showroom, so we started boogieing to the Doobie Brothers and ended up in embrace. Obviously she was smitten by the Good Samaritan type; I was fucked up, horny, and smitten by long legs, tight butt, and bouncing nipples. Nakedness seemed in order, and without a seating area, couch, or other fuckable type surface, I picked her up as I stood there and set her gracefully on my dick. I do not know who was more surprised (it was a first time position for me), but the spontaneity of the moment caught us both up in novel ecstasy, and we bounced to the music with her arms around my neck and my hands firmly grasping her ass cheeks. I swear the fish stopped swimming, gawked and glowed brighter, given the understandably primeval nature of what was before them.

"I must remember this move," I thought to myself as she suggested we move upstairs, and without losing contact of the most intimate connection, I carried her upstairs and gently laid her on her mattress on the floor in the corner. I guess we were into experimental sex, because nothing we did from then on resembled the sort of traditional variety of sucking and fucking so common on the college campuses of America, at least not the ones I had been a part of for the last few years. I remember the amazing shock of lying sixty-nine-like with her toe sensually up my ass. It was on that day that the weird and sometimes awkward realization stuck indelibly in my brain that one's asshole is a sex organ. Ah, the things one learns working on his doctorate. Viva la summer school!

The next morning, I dropped Tracy off at class, attended my two, and with nary a glance to the library or the Baker Center, headed back to Meigs County and The Country Place to take a dip in the pond, feed the animals, and ready the farmhouse for the pending arrival of summer roommates, two friends from undergraduate days, one heading out from Kansas and one coming back to school after a tour of duty in the Marines. So very opposite, but amiable, the Hip and the Captain were about to descend upon The Country Place.

Chapter 4: The Iron Men

you are fair-haired your lips are red
you like softball and the grateful dead
why am i attracted to
the body and the mind of you
      (Joan Baez, "Lucifer's Eyes")

Greg and I had roomed in an apartment in Ft. Worth as undergraduates, just down the street from Pascal High School, home to the imaginary but utterly real football hero (Billy Clyde Puckett) of author Dan Jenkins's irreverent sports novel fame. I would go off to anti-war protest rallies and Greg would go to his Marine meetings. Yea, it seems a little incongruous, but beer-drinking, chasing women, and even some common academic interests kept us friends. When you bond as buddies buying a case of little wine bottles about six ounces each nestled in a Coke bottle like carton of twenty-four for under $8.00 total, drop your dates off at the dorms by curfew (or as the Dean of Women said at one public forum debating the university women's curfew hour of 11:00 pm on weekdays and 1:00

am on weekends, "if you can't get the little thing in by then, you're just not going to do it"), head in his old Nash Rambler to Amon G. Carter Stadium parking lot, and sit there in the front seat with the wine carton between you and discuss matters of the heart and head (including the one in our pants), solve the world's problems, and generally get more honest the more fucked up you get, there is not much pomp and circumstance in a good friendship. When someone knows every detail of every sexual act with every female you've ever slept with, it tends to create a bond as deep as the old adage that "he is someone you'd ride the river with," meaning entrust your life to.

Anyway, he was to begin a master's in economics the next week, and after the rigors of being an officer in the Marine Corps, The Country Place offered total contrasting, non-authority respite. Simultaneously arriving from the plains of Kansas was another college colleague. Dave, or Hip as we called him, came to TCU as a freshman when I was a senior. We were exactly the same size, I mean exactly: 6'3", 185 pounds, size 12 shoe, 36 x 34 pants, and extra large shirts (16 x 35). Well, except his head was bigger. We bonded playing hoops, discussing Dr. Ferre's philosophy classes, organizing anti-war protests, and him lusting after my then current girlfriend, a blond bombshell of a babe who could have been Miss Texas if she had wanted to fuck the pageant higher-ups instead of me. Hip was as bright as anyone who had walked the earth, with an anti-authoritarian personality to match. Technically, he probably could have been classified by the official mental health diagnostic manual as having "anti-social" behaviors, but rarely did such leanings keep him from being charming (particularly with the ladies), intellectually engaging, and an all-around fun guy to hang out with.

Greg took the only bedroom downstairs, Hip used the couch in the living room and kept his stuff unobtrusively stacked in the corner. No one knew how long he might be staying, for as a free spirit, he was known to drift around to where the rent was free, the food good, and the chicks plentiful. He had an open-ended sabbatical from the bike shop where he was the crack mechanic, and living in the country with friends was a better gig than living at home in small town Kansas, albeit with his quite charming mom and grandma. Hip, although intellectually gifted, never could quite suck it up enough and stomach the bullshit of academia to graduate from college, but that never deterred his insatiable appetite for lifelong learning. Anyway, with Hip around, one never had to worry about rolling joints, for out of nowhere he would produce a perfectly rolled tight doobie, get that boyish and slightly mischievous smile on his face, hand it to you, and flick his Bic. How many times did we sing the dope-smoking ditty as prelude to getting all fucked-up?

> In the first days of this country when the buffalo roamed the land,
> All the saddle tramps and cowboys used to roll their own by hand.
> Well they'd swing up to the saddle on their ass or on their horse
> And recite a little ditty that went like this of course.

> When your feet are in the stirrups and your ass is on the ground
> 'Cause the grass that he's been eating is the finest stuff around
> Well let us not remember boys and let us not forget
> Strike a match and light another marijuana cigarette.
> (Jay Ungar, "Strike a Match and Light Another")

Greg had a Saturday orientation in the Economics Department, and Hip and I had a date with destiny, as the cliché would have it, for we were headed off to my first Varmit softball game. Pleased to partake in a little intramural competition, I put on a pair of church league softball pants with an orange strip down the side from yesteryear I'd found in a box of my souvenirs. I topped it off with a clean T-shirt and even had an old pair of soccer shoes with rubber knoblike cleats partially worn, but baseball appropriate nonetheless.

Well, softball "game" was actually a misnomer; the operative word was "games" as all of Saturday would be consumed in legendary feats of softball skill at the Dust Bowl, Meigs County's answer to Yankee Stadium. We retraced our route to Carpenter, but instead of turning right past my tree, we took a left out west on Route 143 to Laura's Corner Store, turned south for a few miles, and nestled off to the east in the forested hills in the heart of Meigs County, there, a softball diamond was carved out of pasture land. It was called the Dust Bowl for really obvious reasons: the infield, bare, rough and rocky, would produce on any given play at any given base a cloud of dust and a hearty Hi-Ho Silver of biblical proportions, so any honest umpire's call on a tag at second base would just have to be taken on faith alone. That did not prevent or remedy the ensuing mandatory arguments that would follow, for competitors need more finite data, and justification by faith just did not seem adequate. The outfield was a pasture, uneven enough to lose a left fielder for short periods of time as he chased a foul ball. But all this aside, it was a functioning ball diamond, with a chain-link backstop, bases, and home to many an enthusiastic softball aficionado.

When Hip and I arrived, we were welcomed not because of our inherent coolness, but more like fresh meat, bodies to fill the positions on the diamond. Little Joe was warming up his pitching arm and Irv was playing catch on the third base side. Other than those fellows, the rest were more than strangers, and they were downright scary. Oh my God, who were these guys? A mangier lot I had never encountered. These were creatures of Rastafarian proportions. Mostly they were shirtless, bearded, with longish, stringy hair, and many shoeless. In fact, the attire of the day consisted of jeans, dirty and holey before hip chicks made it a fashion statement, either long or cut-offs, shirtless chests glistening in the sun, although dirty T-shirts rounded the ensembles of some, and shoes were optional, with only a couple of the Varmits wearing real baseball shoes. Were these locals who had forsaken the ways of their parents, who were probably coal miners, farmers, or common laborers around these parts? Did any of these guys go to college? Have families? Read? Who were they? What had I gotten myself into? "Oh well," I thought. Little did I know that my personal inherent philosophy of "Be here now and embrace the moment" (so popularized by Fritz Pearls, Baba Ram Dass, and pop philosophers of the day) would throw me into a culture from another planet.

"Which one of you is the new guy that lives over by Joe and Irv?" I heard an average framed guy with a scraggly beard ask.

"Well, that's both of us, but I'm the one who has already met 'em," I replied.

"My name is Bob. You two better get warmed up," he instructed.

He shook our hands and turned around to attend to other duties.

The Dust Bowl was built by the Columbia Township Hellcats, another Meigs County softball team that served as the perennial opponent for the Varmits. To say the Varmit softball team was scraggly is definitely an understatement. They had a proud but unenviable history of losing twenty-seven straight games to the Hellcats and others over the past year or so, a record still bragged about today. That was all about to change.

Bob came up again, and I was beginning to surmise that he acted as the Varmits' de facto coach. He eyed my glove and asked if I played first base. It was really more of a statement than a question, given the fact that I was wearing a first baseman's mitt—the only kind I ever owned. So off to first base I trotted. Hip was in the outfield and the Hellcats were up to bat.

During the course of the marathon day of softball, I met many of the other Varmits. Harry lived on the curve in Carpenter in a house I had already passed by several dozen times. My Catawba tree seemed to shade his house, although it was almost a block away. Lou was an infielder and, as I came to find out later, the brother of Tweeter, with whom I had briefly spoken on my investigative visit to Little Joe's place. Tweeter was a sometimes right-fielder, but mostly a score-keeper, and an essential team member throughout the season. Minibaugh was Bob's brother, having acquired the nickname when he was introduced as Bob's little brother sometime in the past and someone yelled, "Oh, he's Minibaugh." Smalley bounced up and shook my hand and all he said was "butt, butt, buddy!" Smalley was short and compact, and in retrospect, he reminded me of the Energizer Bunny. Always quick to laugh, slow to judge, life's problems just did not seem to settle on his shoulders. Michael was the left-handed catcher, the first I'd ever seen, with long, reddish-blond hair, a giant, rounded full beard, and built compact, close to the ground, muscular and quite catcher-like. He was the sometimes caretaker of the field by the fact his farmhouse was a couple of hundred feet from home plate, along with being husband to Delia and father to their toddler, Chugi. Before I knew all this, I eyed a curly-headed blond woman in jean short-shorts and a bra-like halter top with fringes hanging down, similar to Cheyenne meets hippie chick. There were of course other girlfriends, non-playing Varmits, with a few kids running around the backstop and baselines to round out this festive and rather unusual gathering. Some of the kids even wore clothes.

I held down first base for thirty-five innings, only a few of which I remembered, even the next day. After each inning the Varmits would refresh themselves with a cold Rolling Rock from the cooler and pass around multiple joints. Thanks to the weed and the beer, our softball skills over the course of the day got better in our brain and worse in reality. The first game was uneventful, and the Varmits lost for the twenty-eighth time. I was catching almost every ball thrown my way, a first for the team I would learn, and, like any performance athlete, inwardly relished the "nice play" and "great catch" accolades offered by my teammates, but outwardly would just nod and act real cool, like it was nothing.

A line drive was hit to Bob playing shortstop. Stabbing the ball backhand, he spun off balance to throw to first. The ball was low and in the dirt down the line toward home plate. In one fell swoop, I backhanded the ball on a tough hop and tagged the runner out. Ah, the satisfaction of the hoots and hollers. The Varmits went crazy. They loved it. Someone yelled out "What a scoop!" Another hollered, "He is THE scoop!" and all followed with chants of "Scoop, Scoop, Scoop!" It continued all day with every tough dig out of the dirt, and I was more than obliged to give them every reason to shout their mantra, "Scoop, Scoop, Scoop!" From that day forward, the Varmits only knew me by that nickname, and ever since I have assumed it with pride.

Loose and bizarre held true for the whole softball intensive day. We played five games, and Hip and I played every inning. They called us the Iron Men, for we drank and smoked with the best of them. I'd take a leak in the non-existent coaching box off first base line, in front of God, the Hellcats, the team, and even Delia. It was the Varmit Way.

Midway through the endless innings of softball, competitive juices and instinct overwhelmed me and I slid into second base on a stretched-out single. Even attired in real baseball pants, the thinness with no sliding pads meant a giant shiner of a scrape on my thigh, and although it did not bleed, it certainly started to burn. I asked the dugout if any First Aid was to be had. Michael said there was some stuff in his bathroom across the road and I could go get it. While we batted, I trotted over to the square and modest house and entered the front door. Finding the antibacterial goo and applying it liberally to my wound, I was headed out the door though the kitchen when it dawned on me that ice might help as well. A refrigerator came to mind, and I spotted one in the corner and went to retrieve some ice. OK, this was a first. A padlock secured the ice-box as chastity belts protected pussy in days of old. More than a crude analogy, since both the fridge and the female genitals are referred to as a "box." Padlocked? Geez, was the kid sneaking in at night and stealing her milk bottles? Maybe marijuana didn't lose its THC content kept cool, and who wants outsiders smoking up or ripping off your stash? Curious, I left for the diamond and wrapped some ice from the cooler in my T-shirt and administered it to the reddish scrape on my hip, just before heading back out to field.

Playing softball does have its moments of reflective leisure, even in the field. Lounging around first base waiting for the batter to hit gives one pause to reflect on the nature of the universe. I watched with a little interest as Delia raised her Indian halter-top and nursed Chugi sitting in a lounge chair not far from the base path. I contemplated what it would be like to live in the country for real, have a lady like that, and raise some kids. Oh man, that didn't last long, but what lingered was the slight horniness that comes from watching a sexy lady serve up a juicy breast for her little one.

The Varmits won a couple of those games. The streak was broken. A new era of Varmit softball was commencing. Little did we know how much it was about to change all of our softball lives and fortunes. Driving home having drunk countless beers and smoked that many joints, I was always thankful, although not realizing it at the time, that Meigs County was one of the most sparsely populated counties in Ohio (a factoid that may have saved my life numerous times). Although on occasion I would pass another car or truck and give it the old finger wave, a practice I learned going out to Uncle Roscoe's farm in northwest Oklahoma rolling along in his Studebaker truck up and down the sandy roads of the rural farmland. Uncle Roscoe did not talk much, actually. I only remember him saying maybe fifteen words the whole time I knew him, and he died peacefully in his rocker years later. So as I'd pass another vehicle, I'd raise my left index finger slightly off the steering wheel and make eye contact with the driver. Few would respond, so I guessed it just wasn't a custom of the hills of Meigs County. What I learned that was more important was never to assume you are alone out there and use the center of the road, for just as certain you'd come up over a hill and need to swerve to miss an oncoming vehicle. It only took a few of those incidents to be resigned with scrapping the brush near the side of the road and making sure I was taking my half out of the right side.

We pulled into the parking lot and staggered up the hill with only one thought: EAT! Greg was home. Hunger motivated every subsequent move, so I roasted up some chicken, put on John Denver, and all of us as newfound roomies in the country sang the song about our farm feeling like a long-lost friend and how it's cool to be "Back Home Again."

Photo by Andy Sylvia

Photo by Andy Sylvia

Photo by Andy Sylvia

Photo by Andy Sylvia

Chapter 5: The Good Ol' Summer Time

End of the spring and here she comes back
Hi Hi Hi Hi there
Them summer days, those summer days
That's when I had most of my fun, back
high high high high there
Them summer days, those summer days
      (Sly Sylvester, "Hot Fun in the Summertime")

Summer at The Country Place began flowing into a type of rhythm, albeit a most unusual routine as it turned out. Early mornings I'd stumble down the steep stairs from my attic bedroom, finding Greg sitting at the table poring over complicated economic models and munching a bowl of Cap'n Crunch cereal, looking more like a little boy than an ex-jarhead scholar. I'd grab some juice and head out to feed the zoo and take the relaxing drive to Athens.

After a couple of classes and a couple of beers at the Union, I'd stop by the wine and liquor store on State Street, buy a couple of bottles of cheap Riunite wine and a case of Rolling Rock, and head back to Meigs County and The Country Place. By that time I had routered a sign with those words and nailed it to a pole right by the parking lot and the little bridge that forded the trickle of a creek that took one up the hill to the open area that housed the chickens in the coop, the geese in a shed, the overflow flotsam and jetsam of life in the very old root cellar, the roomies in the farm house, the stocked trout in the pond, and the soon-to-be prevalent veggies in the garden.

One cannot live in the country and not have a garden. Now did I know how to plant a garden? Nope, not the first thing. But know-how is not the only tool in one's epistemology, sometimes it is who you know that can lead you down the path you wish to go. And I knew just the right person. Raised as a West Virginia farm boy and spoiled by countless older sisters, Rick was a colleague who started the doctoral program the same day I did. He had graduated with honors from the local college, the renowned Thundering Herd of Marshall, married his college sweetheart, and to avoid the draft, joined the Air Force as an officer and spent some time baby-sitting missiles in Montana, a pretty plum job considering the Vietnam War was still drawing soldiers to its jungles.

"I need to plant a garden at The Country Place," I said casually one afternoon on the porch of the Baker Center drinking beer.

"What do you know about planting a garden?" he replied.

"Oh, having grown up in Oklahoma around good farm folk, I used to eat fresh garden veggies now and then," I bragged.

"Like I said, do you know the first thing about putting in a garden?"

"Well, I thought you'd help me and we'd split the spoils of our labor," I said.

He was more than willing to fall for the slightly Tom Sawyer-like plea. He did, in fact, know all about "putting in a garden," and was not shy to brag about his prowess in that area of expertise, among many others.

"I'll be out early on Saturday morning and we'll prepare the soil and plant. You need to block out a space and get rid of the sod before then. Buy some seeds of the stuff you want to plant and I'll get some starts of tomatoes, peppers, cucumbers, and we'll have the best garden in three counties," Rick confidently instructed. That's how he talked, felt, and lived. I was never sure what his always-confident being was hiding, but I know he surely was confident, bordering on just being a cocky ass. Yet, in many decades, I discovered he rarely blew smoke, and the cockiness was almost always backed up by action, hard work, brilliance, and accomplishment. If I was going to learn how to garden, I got the Monet of West Virginia as my partner.

So for two laborious afternoons after classes, I scooped up sod shovel-by-shovel, wheel-barrowed it out back of the house, and dumped it down the slope to become part of nature in another spot. Mickey and Anise once had a garden there, but I expanded it, and with the expansion came more rocks, but still fine soil. My blistered hands, sore back, and aching arms and shoulders all greeted Rick early Saturday morning when he drove up with tools, a power tiller, plant starts, and his everlasting confidence.

Early Saturday morning had a dramatically different definition for a suburban kid who knew that the good cartoons didn't start till 9:00 a.m., and a West Virginia farm boy who had the cows milked by 6:00 a.m. The master/slave relationship became clear very quickly. But it was a role I fulfilled comfortably, for Rick instructed while he worked, setting a torrid example for my tortured body to mimic. Following his orders was as comfortable for me as working with my older brother, another learned mentor. Somewhere and somehow in my deepest sub-consciousness, I came to the conclusion that I liked Rick because his friendship did in fact feel like my relationship with my older brother.

Who could not like a guy who, only a few weeks after I met him, came to a Halloween party with his office mate, a guy named Rich, costumed as the Boobsie Twins? Strapped to their chests (as they were tied together as well) were two gigantic paper mache breasts, boobs as the case may be, giant flesh-colored tits, with darkened nipples right smack dab in the middle for all to gawk. It takes balls to come to a Halloween party with your fellow grad students and a number of professors and their wives (no, not spouses) as the Boobsie Twins. Without detail, please note the breasts seemed fair game for fondling and, for one out-of-control student, licking. Of course, I came as Snow White, resplendent in platinum wig, knee-length skirt, blouse billowing with breasts of my own making, an extra large bra stuffed with T-shirts. It was the idea of a number of women in our program who wanted to come as the Seven Dwarfs, with pants belted around their knees, shirts tucked in there as well, and funny masks rounding out the bizarre extra big "dwarfs." I looked like a really ugly French whore; they like short-legged lumber jacks.

But I digress. Meanwhile, back in the garden, we roto-tilled, raked, removed rocks, amended the soil with cow and chicken shit, hoed rows, planted seeds, covered seeds, set starts, created mounds for pumpkins and squash, watered, labeled the rows with seed packages on stakes, drank a few beers, and, toward evening, stood leaning on hoe and shovel and admired our handiwork. I learned to plant the beans among the corn because they traded nutrients and the corn stocks became nice climbing "poles" for the beans, and it was a good use of space. I learned to plant squash in mounds, and potatoes in long rounded-up soil rows and to make sure the tomatoes got plenty of the best sunlight. I only learned later in the summer that one should not plant a whole packet of zucchini seeds in one of those mounds; it became an endless object of ridicule by Rick and others when the log-sized zucchini overran The Country Place. I had a stack of those suckers piled up equivalent to two cords of wood, and after a while the geese grew so tired of them they were left untouched when tossed into the pen, at first for their nutrition but ultimately for just pissing them off. So between rotting zukes and a plethora of goose shit (did you know that geese shit five times their body weight every day?), that part of the yard remained quite ripe all summer.

But my heart was right. It knew I needed a garden in my life. When the seeds began to sprout in a few days, the tomatoes began to flower, the first squash blossoms began to appear, the peppers began their tiny birth after little white flowerets, and later when the corn tasseled out, even long before our labor reached full fruition, I'd weed with pure joy, anticipated excitement, and eager readiness for all that was about to abound. I loved to be a part of things that grow, and the depths of my being somehow became more whole with a growing garden just steps out the farm house door.

Hip would go into Athens with me in the morning and work in the library letting innate curiosity guide him to discoveries of the head and his lust for sexy women guide his need for head. Somehow his boyish good looks, sparkling eyes, and clichéd charms seemed to always work. It was never a wonder how successful his reconnaissance radar worked for honing in on and capturing his object of prey. Today was no different. I came out of the INCO building mid-afternoon to meet him for a ride back to the country and there were two coeds, one on each arm. Still undergraduates, one was tall, one was short, and both were built like brick shithouses as we used to say. Hip feigned shyness and said these gals were into some beer drinking, dope smoking, and some of my gourmet country cooking. Hip had extolled the virtues of my immense culinary talent, the extent of which consisted of a mother who was a great cook plus the fact that my first three hours of graduate credit at TCU came from the Home Economics Department in a course called Gourmet Cooking for Men, offered by a fairly cool older home economics professor who grew weary of teaching ditsy Texas belles from small towns around the state and wanted some men and variety in her life, or, at least that is what I speculated as her student. Now those were the days. It was, ironically, Hip's favorite chemistry prof who became his dope-smoking buddy and became our guest lecturer in the class one evening and taught us how to hustle chicks by not adding a toothpick to the olive in the Martini so your date would have to drink the whole thing in order to get the olive to eat, the obvious object of Martini imbibing. The feminist movement, gaining a head of steam in the late 1960s, had not made it to a small church-related school in Texas and certainly not the male species associated therewith. So what could I say to Hip's request: "I have to study"?

Off we roared, with our usual stops for cheap wine, a case of Rolling Rock, and chatty chicks in the back seat thinking this all quite adventurous.

The beer-drinking and dope smoking need not wait for our destination, so by the time we got to The Country Place we were well on our way toward partying hardy. I showed the two lovelies around the place, the chicken coop, the garden, the root cellar, the pond, and the old farmhouse. I got some grub going in the oven and not to let tradition wane, Hip and I asked the coeds if they would like to go swimming in the pond, as we had been doing for days. For whatever reason, shyness, fear, dread of messed-up hair, periods, improper swimming attire, they declined. So Hip and I jumped buck and trotted up the hill to the pond and enjoyed our daily dip. After a few minutes, with a big ol' doobie burned up and feeling no pain, we realized our clothes were down the hill, our towels were in the house, and there was no easy way out of this slight dilemma. So, in the spirit of Butch Cassidy and the Sundance Kid, we spontaneously bolted off the hill, running at top speed to keep from falling, with schlongs flying in the breeze, wet hair trailing behind, yelling joyous utterances and expletives. Maybe it was not a good decision to run directly at the young and now seemingly innocent coeds, but that is what we did. They must have wondered what the fuck these guys were doing, with all our height and weight of naked, running, screaming, possibly very dangerous bodies gyrating right toward them. Here they were, a long way from civilization, with no sure signs of safety or deliverance and two wild men hurdling their bodies and flying body parts directly at them. With thought, I am sure I could have mustered the empathy to see it from their point of view, but they hurriedly declined dinner, and asked Hip to take them back to the dorm. I ate alone, and upon Hip's return, we concluded that we'd remove from our radar girls that were just too young, not adventurous, and certainly all show and no go.

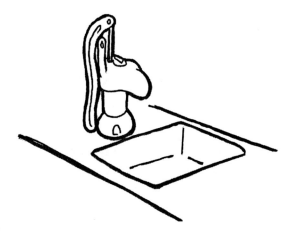

Needing refreshment, back in the kitchen I went for a good head soak of cold well water from the pump on the cabinet next to the sink. Giving it the old rocker arm pumping motion I awaited, like Helen Keller before she had language to describe it, the cool water. Water, two-thirds of the earth's surface, subject of wars, frozen for iced tea, steamed for locomotives, hot for soothing showers, and cold for naked skinny dipping in the mountains streams of the Rockies. Water, necessary for life on earth for all creatures, a great percentage of the earth's surface, carver of canyons, rounder of boulders, mover of sands, flooder of farms and families. Water, gentle as rain and harsh as a hurricane. It's moisture, dew, sweat, fog, showers, ice, falls, glaciers, icebergs, snow, sleet, hail, steam, vapor, mist, and drizzle. It relentlessly seeks its lowest level, and is the cause of rot, damage, rust, and decay. Water is the enemy of oil, wine, and chocolate. It serves as the carrier of deadly diseases, amoeba, protozoa, dirt, trees, sand, cars, bodies, while being the essential life force of us all. Our bodies are mostly water, we crave it, drink it, bath in it, have babies in it, swim in it, and use it for a hundred thousand things. But no water sprung forth from the spout of the pump before me. So with no knowledge of the mechanics of a pump, I grabbed a screw-driver and wrench and began to ply the inner workings of a dysfunctional water delivery system.

Hand pumps use human power and mechanical advantage to move fluids from one place to another. They are widely used in every country in the world for a variety of industrial, marine, irrigation and leisure activities. There are many different types of hand pumps available, mainly operating on a piston, diaphragm, or rotary vane principle with a check valve on the entry and exit ports to the chamber operating in opposing directions. Most hand pumps have plungers or reciprocating pistons, and are a positive displacement. This one was one of those for sure. Come to find out, a leather gasket doesn't last forever, and this one needed replacement.

I loved that pump, and just as I romantically basked in the antique glory of an ancient pump right there in the kitchen, I also developed disgust for its temperamental nature, often needing me to take it apart, massage its innards, replace a part now and then, so that, for a while, happy and cool water would spring forth from its iron spout. But at an early age, I was developing the notion that plumbing was never a fall-back occupational option for me. It wouldn't be a butt crack that would get me fired; but countless utterances of "Oh shit, fuck this shit, and just give me a fucking break" would seal my fate and send me seeking other employment. Water becomes priority number one on the farm. Without it you are doomed; with it, you are nourished and refreshed, and it brings life-giving sustenance to the land, trees, plants and animals. During my stay at The Country Place, I would not only keep the pump in working order, but would also have the cistern pumped out, and water brought by a large tanker truck to replenish the reservoir when the hot summer depleted our water supply. It is a little disconcerting to have muddy water sprout forth from all spigots in the house. But water maintenance, that is, the maintaining of a supply of fresh and potable water, consumed time and energy and remained a high priority throughout my country stay.

The roosters on the place were driving us crazy. If they would have waited till dawn to crow, I think we might have learned to coexist, but they were driving the chickens crazy, too. Not too many people in the world are privy to how chickens fuck. Less know whether it is even essential to egg production, but nonetheless, the horny roosters were on a let's-get-it-on tirade with those poor egg-bearing, feathered creatures as victims. Roosters attack from the rear, and in a flurry of feathers and loud squawking, the hen runs to escape as the rooster runs faster to fuck. The connection lasts for about three seconds on a good day and it is over. The rooster proudly struts away looking satisfied and the hen shies away wondering what happened. It is not much different with other fowl. Upon not knowing what each animal is thinking, and anthropomorphizing their feelings and intentions, as humans we are left with slight shock, a little comedy, and some bewilderment. Fowl fucking is a violent act, from our perspective.

So to cull the tribe of roosters, and enjoy a little outdoor BBQ, we decided to use Mickey's 22-like rifle and go bird hunting, and bag us a few of those loud, obnoxious, horny bastards. Whoa, were we set for adventure. Lots of our hard-earned taxes went to train Greg, now affectionately nicknamed Captain Crunch, for both his Marine officer status and his choice of breakfast food. Why he was an expect marksman certified by none other than the U.S. Marine Corps, who only need a few good men and we had one. So with pride in our armed forces, and a clear order in my voice, I said, "Captain Crunch, commence to fire at will and bag us a bounty of boy birds for dinner tonight." About that time Hip appeared out of nowhere, his specialty, and with little fanfare, lit a joint and passed it around. Captain, after a drag, commenced to fire and effectively chased that scared rooster around the yard, with no deadly impact. Madness ensued, with squawking geese, roosters running around like chickens with their heads cut off (not a good analogy given our intent), Cranfield barking, the cats nowhere to be seen (maybe the only smart creatures

49

on God's green earth), the egg-laying chickens so confused that they didn't know whether to poop, run, or lay go an egg, so they just scurried around and squeaked in a high pitched fearful voice. After witnessing a few minutes of farm chaos, I turned to the Captain and said, "If we are going to make a rifle range free-for-all out of dinner acquisition, we may as well treat this like the circus it appears to be and let me step up to the shooting gallery and give it a pull."

"Here Hot Shot. If you think you can do it any better, fire away," he sarcastically replied.

When things had settled down a little I toked a long drag on the doobie, took a deep breath to relax myself like I was shooting a game-winning free throw, and took aim across the yard to an unsuspecting rooster standing still about fifty yards away on a little knoll.

Deftly I slowly pulled the trigger, and it surely was the second shot heard round the world, for that bird did nothing but wilt instantaneously to the ground, cold-cocked and deader than a doornail. Of course nobody believed the causal relationship between my shot, the bullet, and the dead bird; they stretched for some explanation of divine intervention to account for such a miracle on the grass. The three of us walked silently across the lawn to inspect the kill. Hip picked the rooster up by the neck and, lo and behold, there was one clean shot directly through the middle of its head, temple to temple. Did I gloat? Of course not. I just turned to the Captain and said that I wanted my tax dollars back, for we had wasted them on training him to be an expert marksman in three weapons. He mumbled something about being lucky but pouted for days.

We actually caught another one and did the gracious thing and chopped off its head on a tree round with an old rusty hatchet. Ah, fresh farm game for dinner. Manly suffering through the smell of wet feather and warm guts, we cleaned and plucked the birds and prepared them for the BBQ. It must be written somewhere, or common knowledge elsewhere, or even a law in some land, or information passed down from generation to generation in some cultures, or conventional wisdom known but unspoken by peoples around the globe, but no, not here, not now, no, no son-of-a-bitch told **me**. These are not your supermarket variety of chicken that come neatly wrapped in cellophane, nestled on Styrofoam trays on little diapers to soak up the blood and bodily fluids so much a part of dead birds. No, these were old roosters, grizzled by mobility, hardened by the outdoor elements, muscled by their multiple daily chicken fuckings, creatures of sinew reminiscence of an old leather shoe, really a very old, tough, stinking, dirty leather shoe. Luckily Rick and Alice could bring some store bought ones, but that only gave Rick an excuse to razz us good, telling us no one eats roosters except by boiling them for twenty-four hours and pounding them into sandwich meat. So now you tell me. "Well, this is how you learn in the country," I thought.

Chapter 6: Porn, Jesus and Iced Tea

The old maroon Chevy Impala began to know the way to Athens by itself. That was a good thing, but knowing the way home was even better. By now the road always traveled via Albany and little Carpenter became a soothing respite, like a sensual back massage. Driving those verdant hills I would often reflect on what it was like 120 years before when the Underground Railroad had several trails through this countryside. In fact, as I learned, just three miles east of Carpenter at the junction of route 143 and 692, not far from Pageville, a safe house or "station" stood serving the loose network of aid to help blacks move toward freedom. The Welsh family, living on a farm near that intersection, helped travelers by night on their way north. About seven different trails converged in Albany, and for decades abolitionists and anti-slavery believers befriended thousands escaping the horrors of slavery in the South. I learned no one knew why it was called the Underground Railroad, for it was neither. But to imagine small groups of people migrating mostly at night and laying low in the daylight across Meigs County, including using rivers like Raccoon Creek, seemed like exotic history to me.

Meanwhile, summer classes clipped along, the garden became lush, the mid-summer Southeast Ohio humidity relegated showers at best temporary if not useless, and the $330-a-month graduate stipend paid the rent, bought the beer and grub, and was enough to buy some toothpaste every once in a while and see a movie at the Athena on Court Street every so often. Being a film fan, I looked forward with relish to the midnight offerings at the Athena every Wednesday night to support the Athens International Film Festival. I'd work in the library till it closed, walk uptown to the Tavern at the far end of Court Street, drink a pitcher or two with some always gathered graduate buddies as we'd badmouth our weird professors and bemoan how much work we had to do.

A few minutes before midnight, Rick and I and whoever else was so inclined, would hop in the old Chevy, light up a big doobie, and create a satisfied state of mind appropriate for the appreciation of our imminent cinematic treat. The place would be packed, male and female, young and old, rich and poor, hillbilly and hipster. Our contingent felt no pain, so for two hours as proud patrons of the arts, we would immerse ourselves in the most recent releases and most famous of porn movies. Yep, that is how the Athens International (excuse me) Film Festival supported itself, admirably I might add. From classics like *Deep Throat*, to my favorite, Marilyn Chambers in *Behind the Green Door*, to totally boring *Debbie Does Dallas*, and running the gamut to lesser known shockers like *Big Ball in Cowtown*, the audience, well lubed with plenty of beer, provided plenty of risqué comments. When some old hairy dude was balling some chick in the ass on a pool table the commentary would be, "ten four back door," and "table that motion, you big dog." It got worse from there. Many of us saw this arts patronage as an essential part of our community involvement and greater graduate education, not to mention the pure prurient interest the lively arts provided and its contributions to a good boner for the trip home.

Other nights were quieter. The country living suited me just fine, with its unbridled energy and moments of meditation, but it was a long way from the surrounds of the Midwest lifestyle of my childhood that brought the comforts of how I defined "home." Food, family, friends, faith, football, and all things Heartland still stirred up yearnings inside and peaked insatiably in my soul. So for grounding in many things, both spiritual and physical, on many an evening, I would wander over to Ben and Weezie's for a big glass of sweet iced tea, and a whole lot more. Ben and I started the Ph.D. program the exact same day, too.

"Howdy, my name is Ben. Nice to meet you," he drawled.

"What part of Texas you from, Ben?" I chuckled back.

"Well, grew up on the coast but just came from Abilene," he responded with more elongated vowels than ever needed in an English sentence.

"I spent some time in Ft. Worth, so I consider myself part Texan."

"Whajado in Ft. Worth, anyway?"

"Went to school there at TCU."

"Oh, I see, those ol' Horned Frogs had a pretty tough year, didn't they?" he said real slow and emphatically.

Now any self-respecting even part Texan knows that line refers to football. If your life in Texas did not revolve around football, you must have been a pervert. Of course other prejudices abound in Texas, a football anti-fan would just as likely be run you out of town on the rails (an act not to be taken lightly) for it happened to many undesirable types in small towns all over Texas, whether your trouble was not embracing football, being black, speaking Spanish, or other unfortunate leanings.

"Yea, we are in a rebuilding decade and hope to be competitive soon," I said, thinking that by the turn of the century maybe we'd win a game or two.

"I went to Baylor a few years back," he revealed.

Now that explained it, for Baylor was a Baptist school down I-35 and a big rival of TCU with its Disciples of Christ heritage. Further south down I-35 lived the Longhorns of the University of Texas at Austin, or, as the burnt orange and white bumper stickers proudly declared, "The University." Not to be outdone, the Baylor Baptists countered with their own reverent and pious bumper moniker: "Thee University." TCU never came up with anything that cute. Still, in spite of our old rivalries, the blood of Texas runs thick, and Ben and I became good friends.

He was a little older than I and a little more conservative, and he took God and Jesus a lot more seriously. Yet, without a doubt, he was, and still is, one of the more wonderful and unusual humans to walk the earth.

The first week of school he invited a bunch of fellow graduates down to his married student housing near the South Green for some appetizers and conversation. With chips and dip and a Coca-Cola satisfied tummy, Ben announced that he had a reason other than social for inviting us up to his apartment.

"I have heard that lots of graduate programs around the country are competitive and students develop mistrust among their cohorts. I just want all of you to know that I plan to be available to anyone if there is anything I might be able to do to help. I will share all my research with you if it might be needed, and I hope to create a collegial relationship with each of you. I just want to have some fun and support each other during our stay here over the next few years."

There was silence for quite a while. What ensued was the magic that can happen when truth is spoken forthrightly. Candor sometimes compels us all to rise to the occasion. And that is what my fellow students did. They committed to supporting each other, and throughout all three years of my graduate education, I do not recall a time when a graduate student usurped that commitment. That was the power of Ben.

He had been married for a few years, taught in college, served Uncle Sam in the Army, and was just older and more mature than many of our colleagues. So when the local Athens Bank asked him for his ID when cashing a check one day, Ben got pretty livid. To some that might not seem like a big deal, but to someone from small town Texas who knew the barber, the filling station attendant, the lady at the cleaners, the butcher, the baker, and the candlestick maker, for a bank, one in which you are a depositor in good standing, to ask for ID was tantamount to ultimate disrespect. Now Ben had on an old worn leather jacket that he loved and he looked enough like a student to be treated like one, but that was not how he wanted to be treated. So the next day, he dressed up in his finest Sunday-go-to-meetin' suit and tie, marched into the Athens National Bank on the corner, and asked to see the President.

"Hi, my name is Ben," he stated as he stuck out his hand to shake the bank President's. He had a quizzical look on his face as he shook Ben's hand.

"Have a seat, Ben. What can I do for you?"

"I just came from Texas and yesterday I came in your bank to transact business and your counter employees were disrespectful to me," Ben began to explain.

"I am sorry that happened Ben, what did they say to upset you," he replied in his best customer-service voice.

"They asked for my ID."

"Hummm, that is common practice here in a college town. We meant no disrespect," he apologetically said. Ben responded quite softly and humbly, true to his style and temperament, saying, "Who I bank with is important to me. I expect that people know me and are friendly to me when I come into my bank, and I wonder how we could make that happen here, if I am to continue doing business with you," he so sweetly threatened.

The President escorted Ben out to the lobby, introduced him to the Vice President, the tellers, the account representatives, and told them that they no longer needed to ask for Ben's ID for he was a customer in good standing.

I do not know what the President of the bank told the tellers after Ben left, and it could have included a good laugh, but months later Ben needed to get me a cashier's check to order some supplies for a research project we were doing, and sure enough, when Ben walked into his bank there was a cacophony of "Hello Bens" that echoed throughout the bank. Other customers turned to look to see the famous person or large investor that was the recipient of all the acknowledgments. Ben just returned the smiles and addressed the teller by name. Just another example of the power of Ben.

It was Ben who recommended me to a guy by the name of John. He was a TV major and served as director of a television magazine format show on WOUB, the public broadcasting affiliate located on campus. He needed a folksy talking host who could be a natural storyteller and introduce guests, interview some, and generally take the show, called "Almanac," to the top of the charts. The focus of the show was on the culture, history, music, arts, and uniqueness of that part of Appalachia. The station's reach included parts of West Virginia, Kentucky, and Virginia, along with southeast Ohio. So with the promise of stardom, I became "talent," as they say in the industry, for a ten-part series of local interest. They wrote the script and I was supposed to follow it and sound natural, like I was just thinking it up and saying it spontaneously. Wow, that didn't work. I was stilted, stiff, and horrible. It is truly humbling to sit in a post-production meeting and be a part of the show's critique, and have most every word, all phrases, glances of the eyes, tilts of the head, and movements of the mouth analyzed in minute detail. Not a fun event. For the next taping, I asked for the script the day before and read the content, walked in and started the show with my own intro: "Howdy, this is Almanac, and we're gonna have some fun today." I saw the heads of the production staff drop in shock.

But if they wanted folksy, then a script just would not work. By the end of the "live on tape" session, people had warmed up to the character on the set, and the post-show critique was not painful but rather enjoyable. I did a location shoot at the Humane Society talking about the county being overrun with dogs and cats and how many they had to kill. I interviewed several visiting artists during the season, including Sonny Terry and Brownie McGhee, a black singing duo in the southern folk and jazz tradition. Months after the season was completed and my TV fame had faded, I learned that national public television picked up that interview and ran it nationally. I never saw the final version.

But like I said, Ben and Weezie grounded me in all things Heartland. By the second year of grad school, they had moved to a little house on Washington Street near campus and settled into a domestic lifestyle. They had a big, nice, and soft white couch, real furniture, a fully-equipped kitchen, running water, and big pillows in the living room for flopping and hanging out. I would drop by to give Ben some recent research and would succumb to Ben's customary invitation to "Come in this house!"

"Oh, OK, just for a little while," I would say having been seduced by the warm welcome.

After solving the problems we had with professors, the school, the country, and the world, Weezie would say I must stay for dinner and eat some tuna casserole. We'd talk about all things important, from school to very personal stuff. They would tenderly question my lifestyle, why I cussed, and what was of importance in my religious beliefs. Although I stretched the limits of their Texas and Christian values, never did I feel judged, and the spiritual quality of their being and their home wrapped me in comfort and love. Between naps on the couch, we'd watch football and eat the wonderful creations that Weezie would so effortlessly produce out of the kitchen. These meals often resembled the casseroles on the table of my childhood. Something inside me needed this respite, where smoking dope was not the norm, only tea and soda were consumed for refreshment, and there were no farm mates to look after and interact with or animals to feed. There were funny stories about how Ben and Weezie got married, or about how they almost didn't get married due to Ben's cold feet at the last minute, and about how Ben became an Army officer almost instantly, and, afterwards, of course, there were reflections on all things Texas.

Rarely would I stay all night, but leaving the confines of their home was never easy. They either just liked me around or knew that I needed spiritual refueling. Another reason would surface that would keep me in their fold for hours, and often late at night I would escape and head back to the country. I'd pass the ol' tree in Carpenter and tell it that I was blessed to have spent some time at the Holy-Sanctified-Church-of-Tuna-Casserole-and-the-Sleepy-Couch with Pastor Ben presiding. The tree stood still but understood. Remember, you are alone in the car, and who's to say the tree does not hear and understand?

It is said that the mark of a mentally healthy individual is one who can handle massive quantities of ambiguity. My ambiguities included the contrast between the town and the country, the university and the lifestyle in Meigs County, the professors and the Varmits, and the respectable student and the outrageous behaviors of the inhabitants of The Country Place. I faced the contrast between the intense intellectualization of my studies and the dogged adherence of the Varmits' respectful anti-intellectualism. There were plenty of chances to test my mental health and to handle a few ambiguities, which, at the time, did not seem like any big deal, and even felt quite natural. Maybe that was the crazy part.

Chapter 7: Ringers, Skinny-dippers, and Victors

After a Sunday of beer, marijuana, sunshine, dust and oh, softball, Bob announced that he had entered us in a softball tournament the following weekend in Athens, sponsored by the local venerable men's institution, the bastion of testosterone, Baron's Men's Shop. It was a remnant of the blue sports jackets with gold buttons, penny loafers, cardigan sweaters, London Fog overcoats, and striped-tie days when "frat rats" and "sore whores" roamed college campuses dressed for every occasion and were as cool and rich as they were well-dressed.

Athens Parks and Recreation had a few softball diamonds in the dike-protected flood plain down by the Hocking River. The event would thus be by the gently flowing water that split the town and university. Luckily, Bob reassured us that he'd fill out our tournament roster with a couple of ringers he knew from back home in Chillicothe. Dubious as I was, we did need warm bodies to fill positions and take a real swing at the plate now and then.

Come Saturday morning I donned my old church softball pants, threw on a clean T-shirt and worn soccer cleats, and headed into Athens. It was a gorgeous day for baseball. The fields were buzzing with teams warming up, but it was not hard to spot the Varmits. This being a tournament did not persuade them to up-tempo their wardrobe any, so scraggly jeans and dirty T-shirts proliferated, but in a bold departure from conventional wisdom, they all had on shoes. It was only later that I learned it was a tournament rule. Harry was one of our pitchers, but given the length of most of the Varmits coiffeurs, maybe they just should have all have been named Harry.

The softball world of America, ubiquitous throughout thousands of communities across the nation, was taken very seriously by its aficionados. It still remained the bastion of All-American boys of all ages. It was as American as Nixon, the Vietnam War, your local VFW Hall, apple pie, the Pledge of Allegiance, and 4th of July picnics in the park. Teams were composed of firefighters, teachers, policemen, fraternity boys, business execs, factory workers, construction guys, and those who held other mainstream, manly positions known and respected across our land. Teams were not usually fielded by social workers, hair stylists, members of the local arts council, community organizers, university professors, or those of any number of less manly occupations of the foo-foo nature. Softball tournaments just were not frequented by protesting, draft-dodging, anti-war, politically-active, liberal-leaning, long-haired, socially degenerate, hippie types. Not until now. Not that the Varmits were all or any of those things, but the perceptual world as it is, you could see the mental wheels a-turning under each matching cap of the opposing team players that took a gander glancing over at us warming up.

I had been to a number of anti-war protest rallies, even organized a few myself, and when the "Love It or Leave" anti-protest folks arrived to counter demonstrate and tensions became edgy, one could drag out the old cliché and state accurately to his buddy standing alongside, "I can feel the tension in the air." I grew up with all of their types, went to church every Sunday, choir every Wednesday evening, was president of the youth group, and chaplain of the student council at an all white suburban high school in Oklahoma City, where every morning on the public address system I would give a little devotion and prayer. The only concession to ecumenicalism was always remembering to not say "In Jesus' Name" at the end like we did in church. I do not know what the atheist, Jews, Muslims, Hindus, Buddhist, or persons of other myriad religious affiliations might have thought, for they were small and powerless, and by-God this was Oklahoma, and Christianity ruled back then and there.

The irony of two of my worlds, one as a Varmit and the other representing the one I grew up in years before, was not lost on me. You just have to picture the contrast. Polyester was king of the 1970s fabric world, and softball uniforms had embraced it as the washable, durable, wrinkle-free cloth of choice. No player had obtained a size larger than he needed, so the stretch of the polyester clung to every curve, indentation, and swoosh of the body, including wrapping around so many with "Dunlop's Disease," where their bodacious beer guts had "done lapped" over their wide black belts circling the loin area. Oh, except for one team that had matching white belts and shoes, quite a fashion statement. Each uniform was exactly the same, except for the number on the front and back. Each uniform was pristinely cleaned, shoes were shined, hat brims had been painstakingly molded to the perfect curve, and each pair of legs had traditional socks cut minutely at mid calf, the style of the day. The ball gloves were groomed with fine leather ointment, and they smelled of English Leather After Shave lotion (the men, not their gloves). Hair did not stick out from under their caps, ponytails did not protrude down their backs, and I'll never know if they wore briefs or boxers, but I would wager a pretty safe bet that they had one or the other, very unlike the Varmits, believers in free-balling as the way to go.

Between the raw humor of the event and the churning in my gut of old tensions of the political nature whelming up inside, I couldn't wait until the heat of the action commenced. But first, the team captains had to meet to lay out the ground rules. I guess they had to make sure we were all law abiding U.S. citizens with passports, and that we met other bizarre requirements of the official softball world. That's when the shit hit the fan. One coach said we could not play because we had no uniforms, one questioned our application, another protested that our balls were dirty (our softballs, that is) and that our bats did not conform to standard, whatever that meant. Folks dragged out rulebooks, the argument grew louder, and one could've divided the coaches right down the middle with the tolerant on one side and the intolerant on the other. A microcosm of cultural and political contrasts and conflicts of our United States was being displayed in all seriousness on the softball field of life, right there in Athens County. Finally the conflict turned to consensus with the "Let 'em play" faction winning the day; everyone merged into agreement because, what could it hurt? These guys weren't going to last very long in the tourney anyway: they'd paid their entry fee, and they would be easy pickings for a quick victory.

Lesser humans would have been offended. But these were guys who had already chosen to be different, to be on the outside, to stick out, and to renounce the real world of systems, rules, social norms, antiquated mores, and law-abiding behaviors.

So when Smalley shouted "Butt, butt, buddy, let's play!" any angers, moping hearts, feelings of oppression, notions of put-downs, and other navel-staring hurts quickly gave way to "Play Ball," the last two words of our national anthem.

Bob introduced the team to our ringers, Chip and Freddy. The tourney power gave us our five minutes of field warm-ups, so as the outfield shagged flies, the infield did their round-robin grounders, outs at first and double plays. Mike played catcher, Paul at third, Chip at short, Lou at second, and the Scoop at first. Paul had a rifle arm from third, and a quick fielding glove on both sides of his body, so there was no surprise when he fielded the first grounder and hurled it perfectly to first. Next came Chip at short, and having never seen this guy until a few minutes before, I was curious what made him so special. Bob had bragged about him being a minor leaguer in the Reds system for a while.

The grounder skittered slightly to his right, and he gracefully moved in front of it before taking a step forward to catch it mid-bounce and, in one fluid motion, rifled the ball to first. I didn't move my glove. It hit dead center, chest high, with a velocity I had not experienced often. This is when I realized baseball tryouts do not have to last long. For pitchers, can they get it over the plate, do they have some stuff, and what does the gun say about their gun? For hitters, a good coach can watch a guy swing the bat a few times, hit a couple of balls, and pretty much know if the kid can play. I watched Skip pick up one grounder and throw to first, and instantly knew that this kid could *play*. It was true in other sports. One could toss a basketball to a kid and by the time he caught it and bounced it on the floor a couple of times, you would know whether there was talent there or not.

During the warm-up, a grounder was hit to Lou at second, and turning a double play, he tossed it to Chip who was barreling down on the bag. The ball scooted in the dirt to his left, and as he reached to pick it up on one hop he headed out to right field. He could not throw to first off balance so he planted his right foot, pirouetted around as in the ballet, and threw a strike to first. I was in such awe of the move, the ball nearly hit me in the face, but I recovered and snagged it at the last second and spun around and tossed it home. I now had the concept of ringer indelibly etched in my brain. But there was more to come.

Our first opponents were the pot-bellied policemen from a town on the Ohio River, with a few recruits and sons thrown in to round out their competitive edge. How could we complain? We had our ringers, too. Depression sets in quickly for me when losing. I hate to lose. It took me years to beat my dad in ping-pong on our table centered in the garage with woodworking tools and stacks of random lumber cleared away just enough to accommodate the table. After routinely whooping my dad, it was on to my older brother, whose five years my senior made him a worthy adversary. I got better than him pretty quickly, but he would pull out the old psychological tricks that would get me so pissed off I'd blow it somehow. Hugh took great pride in his mental prowess and giving me shit, but I learned some mental toughness of my own, and began beating him regularly, with only his brush-off that I was lucky. That went on for a couple of years before our games ended when he went away to college.

The Varmits were staring the consolation bracket in the nose. Down three runs at the top of the seventh inning with last at bat, I had that deep-sinking feeling balled up in my gut that we were going to lose. We had not hit the ball very well, we'd made stupid errors in the field, and we probably did not deserve to win. But destiny might just have had other plans, we hoped. Lou grounded out. By some miracle, I chopped a high-bouncer between second and third and got on base. Bob followed with a blooper to right, so we had two runners on and still just one out. Chip was up and, watching him from second, I just knew this guy was a hitter. His pre-batting routine was natural and showed years of rehearsal. He dug the perfect hole to plant his back foot, took just the right amount of dirt to rid his hands of sweat, and gently swung the bat back and forth before readying it in the cocked position behind his head. A high-lob throw of slow pitch softball fame dropped low and inside, around Chip's knees. In one power chop, looking more like a golf swing than a baseball one, he launched a ball toward left field that looked like it was going to circumnavigate the globe. I was ready to run if caught, not likely since the left-fielder, had he been able to track it down, would have been so deep that the curvature of the earth would not have allowed him to see third base, so I thought it a good bet I could tag and make it. The ball landed around second base of the adjacent diamond, hundreds of yards from home plate.

"Foul ball!" the umpire yelled.

"Straighten it out, Chip," I said. It was always the mark of a genius to state the obvious. Chip fouled another pitch off and now he was down 0-2. My gut was acting up again, telling me that losing was imminent. The third pitch was calculated to be a sucker pitch, just on the outside corner of the plate to risk being called a strike, but not a real pretty pitch to hit. That notion was not lost on Chip, and he was not taking any chances. His left foot stepped toward the plate and with an upper cut of monstrous proportions he crushed the ball. I mean tore the cover off of it. I mean smashed a towering drive to right field that had nothing but "out-of-here" etched all over it. I knew at impact, and leisurely began my trot to home plate. Hope springs eternal in the human breast (as Keats used to say) and now it was a tie game and anything could happen. Paul grounded out and with only one out left, Freddie was up. He had already struck out twice (not an easy feat in slow pitch softball), so confidence did not overwhelm me. Freddie was not very tall, but had shoulders of someone eighteen inches taller, a narrow waist, and arms like cannons, as is clichéd. In fact, he was often called the "Toy Cannon" as an appropriate nickname. He was built like the proverbial brick shithouse. He was quiet, stoic enough to be considered anti-social. He glided into the batters' box and unassumingly took his stance.

"Strike one," the umpire hollered.

"Well, I guess Freddie just didn't like that one," I leaned over and whispered to Irv. The Varmits were all yelling, "Come on Freddie, you're the one Freddie," and other words of encouragement.

I had never seen a stance quite like his: hunched over real low to make an infinitesimally small strike zone and leaning back so far as to run the risk of falling into the catcher's lap. Although mostly upright, he seemed more coiled to strike than ready to swing a bat. The next pitch must have been to his liking, for it had barely left the pitcher's hand when Freddie cocked back, kinda shook the bat slightly above his head, and waited. It wasn't exactly a swing, more like the uncoiling of a spring, the powerful strike of a rattlesnake biting its prey, the deep drawback of a bow and arrow and its release, or a catapult held in place by a rope that now has been cut and let loose in a fury of vengeance, and all of that power was directly focused on the grapefruit-sized spheroid softly floating down toward home plate. The swing was as unorthodox as it was mighty, and to this day it must still be a hazard to satellites circling the planet. The ball was gone. Oh yea, pandemonium did break out on the Varmit side, while our nattily dressed opponents stood in stark silence. You'd thought we'd just won the World Series against the Yankees, hand-slapping, shucking and jiving, dancing and hugging, and more than enough "butt, butt, buddies" to go around. We'd come back from the brink of defeat, snatched victory from the horrors of that suffering, and would continue in the winners' bracket later that afternoon.

But now it was time to eat, drink, smoke, relax, and relive the game play by play, in Varmit style. Smalley suggested we grab some sandwiches and beer and go cool off at a swimming hole. A bunch of Varmits piled in the old Chevy, and we headed to a little grocery store to acquire the beer, chips, bread, meat, and cheese, and off we went. Where? I did not know. Everyone seemed clear of the exact location of this swimming hole, so since I was driving, I asked.

"Oh Scoop, just drive out past Carpenter on 50 and we'll show you."

Sure enough, not far from the Vinton County line I was instructed to turn right on 43B and a mile or two back into the woods Tweeter tells me to take a left on an unmarked road. Dead ahead a few hundred yards was a classic old covered bridge, but barricaded to not allow car traffic.

"Just park right in front of the bridge," said Tweeter. I got out of the car and walked around to the side of the road and viewed the stream meandering below the bridge. Downstream, the trees arched in a giant canopy of green lushness. Smalley patted me on the back and said, "Welcome to Varmit State Park, Scoop. Let's go cool off, Dude."

Little did I know that the Varmits had their own state park, acquired, like many of their other possessions, by proxy and acquisition. This was their adopted swimming hole, and, at that time in my life, one of the most beautiful places I'd ever seen on earth. Raccoon Creek was clear, tumbling over rocks and ebbing into eddies of calm, with the welcome shade trees like a huge natural nave of a sixteenth century European cathedral overhead. The antique bridge now behind us, I stood there in awe. The majesty was stunning. You could not say the Varmits did not have good taste: this spot was special. Other cars began arriving, joints were passed, food was laid out on the big rocks by the creek, and clothes were handily abandoned.

Naked bodies glistened in the sun everywhere. The most decadent (a tough determination) of the Varmits had already positioned themselves in the water cascading around the rocks and, when just right, got a constant neck massage of cold bubbles. I swam around in a little pool about four feet deep and, as the dust of the ball field floats downstream to replenish the riparian beds of the stream bank I overheard numerous conversations about our victory, our ringers, and our afternoon opponents. The Varmit ladies prepared food, and took relaxing dips of their own. Paul was off to the side of the stream having a conversation with his lady, a young woman by the name of Nancy.

He walked over to get some grub and that's when I noticed Nancy for real. She was slowly and deliberately taking off her top, unbuckling her jeans, and pulling them down over her ass and off each leg. Now I tried to be nonchalant, but my eyes could not stray for one second from what was before me. She turned away from us to face the bridge and glided her panties off her butt, slipped off each sock, and pinned her hair up in back. Her skin was pure and white; no tan lines obscured its ivory smoothness. She probably weighed all of 110 pounds, and like many twentyish coeds stood there unassumingly unabashed in all her nubile glory, with pointy tits arching toward the sky and the sensual curve of her waist sending chills up and down my spine and other body parts (thank heaven for cold water). She carefully traversed the rocky water's edge and slithered in like a graceful mermaid. I was transfixed, but I tried to be cool and not notice. She swam up to Paul and they exchanged loving, splashy greetings, and since they were now quite near, Paul introduced me to his lady.

"This is Scoop, our new first baseman. Scoop, this is Nancy, my lady."

Now what do you say to a naked goddess standing before you in the stream of life? I muttered something creative and original like, "Hey, Nancy, how are you?" All the while, thinking how important it was to remember to look at something besides her breasts bobbing just above the water line. So I said to myself, "Look at her eyes, look at her eyes!" Oh was that a mistake, because as her body embodied pure sensuality, her eyes were the spoken invitation of the Sirens. They were not only inviting, but longingly lonely and spoke volumes. Classic bedroom eyes, they softly asked to be kissed and were fiery enough to hint at a secret message: "And I want to turn you every way but loose." For distraction and enjoyment, strains of the Grateful Dead flowed through my mind as the cool water bubbled past my bones.

Sugar Magnolia blossom's blooming
Head's all empty and I don't care

Saw my baby down by the river
Knew she'd have to come up soon for air

Sweet blossom come on under the willow
We can have high times if you'll abide
We can discover the wonders of nature
Rolling in the rushes down by the riverside

She's got everything delightful
She's got everything I need
A breeze in the pines in the summer night moonlight
Crazy in the sunlight yes indeed
        (Robert Hunter and Robert Weir, "Sugar Magnolia/Sunshine
Daydream")

How much of that entirely non-verbal eye messaging was really in her eyes or in my fantasies, who knows, and really, who cares? But she was Paul's lady, and I, a below-the-Mason-Dixon Line southern gentleman, with respect and deference, made small talk and would never even think about hustling another man's woman, well, except if the opportunity presented itself to me. Lust can only hope. Anyway, I could ask myself, "What would the Varmits do?" and find moral guidance from that sincere questioning. If you don't know the answer to that question yet, rest assured, it will be answered within these pages before long.

I heard Irv giving the play by play of our recent victory upstream a little and swam over to listen.

"Hey, nice hit, ah, if that's what you call it, Scoop." Irv chided. Everybody laughed, but a mild feeling of belonging came with my smile, one that is created in manly battle, team sports, and masculine bonding experiences. Just then a rousing chorus of the Varmit theme song started a medley of rounds, "I'd rather smoke, smoke, smoke than work, work, work. I'd rather screw, screw, screw, than work, work, work." The possibilities of a verse about something being better than work were endless, and our laughter and singing was only interrupted when Bob yelled out, "It's time to head to Athens!"

Food was gathered up, dirty clothes were repositioned on wet bodies, and cars were loaded as we worked down the last of the roaches, ready to do battle with another polyester clad look-a-like team of the American Right.

Word got around the tournament that the Varmits had won a game, stirring up the intolerants' arguments that they should never have let us play. So when we hit our groove in game two and won handily that afternoon, the buzz around the stands, at the hot dog cart, and among the teams was almost audible. To the credit of the Varmits, they were just as good winners as they were losers, a much more practiced position. We were friendly, gracious, and never said disparaging things to the other teams. I cannot say we were winning the hearts and minds of all, but like a town embracing and protecting its own local "town idiot," as they were not so appropriately called back in the early days of the twentieth century, the Varmits were being embraced as a novelty, as one would embrace a mangy ol' pet.

Our ringers amazed. Freddie raced down flies in the outfield long given up for a hit or a foul ball. Any ball from behind third base or near center field was devoured up by Skip with many a surprised look on the runners' faces when they realized I had started the ball around the infield as they were approaching the first base bag. The ugly duckling was being transformed before our very eyes, for the ringers raised the level of play of us all. With two wins under our beltless jeans, and two or three games on Sunday to win it all, it was Saturday night in Athens and time to party. That day, I learned that the Varmits not only had their own State Park, but also their own bar, Harpo's. Few college types made it down the hill to frequent this bar because it catered more to locals and ne'er-do-wells. So when our entourage piled into Harpo's we loudly filled the place, ordering pitchers of beer and greasy grub from the kitchen. Between piss breaks at the stinky john in the corner and doobie breaks around back by the trash, we pretty much stayed focused on drinking and back slapping.

Well on our way to beer-induced nirvana, the depth charge challenge sat before me on the table of excess. The depth charge challenge goes like this: shots of whiskey are dropped into a glass almost full of beer and you try to drink the beer, without using hands, before the shot glass hits bottom, which is well after you do, I would soon learn. I was told the next day that I did manage driving the car to deposit a few Varmits at their respective abodes, but all I remember was saying to myself, "Do not drive into the house, do not drive into the house, do not drive into the house." Now why that was important is anybody's guess, because I could have driven into a thousand other things along the back roads of Meigs County, so upon awakening the next morning, actually a miracle in itself, I was not surprised to stumble into the sunlight and notice the car carefully parked about six inches from the house.

"How'd the car get parked so close to the house?" Hip inquired.

"Well, I was pretty drunk and didn't want to have to walk too far," I said.

Being a finely-tuned athlete and in serious training for the softball season, I realized there was just enough time to wolf down my Wheaties and head into Athens for the tournament finales. Three aspirins were my hope for abating the booming headache. With a banana to replace potassium, I was good to go and fit as a fiddle, so to speak. Four teams were left in the winners' bracket: us, Baron's, and a couple of out-of-town teams. You had to win the semi-finals, and then if you won the finals, you had to beat the consolation team once to win it all. If you lost that, you had to play a final playoff game. That means a team could theoretically play four games on Sunday to vanquish the last of the winners bracket and the only remaining team from the loser's bracket.

Game three was not pretty, but workmanlike. We won by a couple of runs, not due to any assistance I could provide. It was going to take a little more sun and time for me to feel up to my Wheaties.

It was just after lunch and the Baron's team was in the finals of their own tournament, against the most unlikely of foes, the Varmits. It was polyester spit-and-polish against the unwashed and uncouth. Frat Rats meet Degenerates. Cool college kids squaring off against country yahoos, the Beaux of the Balls facing the free-balling boys of Meigs County. This was epic at many levels: Americana, social classes, fashion choices, hairstyles, values, and the cheering supporters of each side. The contrast on the field was only surpassed by the juxtapositions in the stands. There on the Varmit side sat our well-wishers: country hippie chicks as wives, girlfriends, wanna-bes, and a few local Meigs County farmers that had to check out the scene. Jean cut-offs, halter tops, bare feet, nursing nipples, unruly hair, and the smoky smells of home cooking and dope. Only a few feet away sat the Baron Bleacher Bitches, sorority gals dressed to the nines. Lacy tops, adorned bra-embraced boobs, hot pants nestled up both front and rear cracks, hair piled in puffed, ratted, and sprayed globs, and the Bitches side of the stands smelled of Chanel No.5, Shalimar, Muguet de Bois, and hairspray. They sat prim and proper, legs together, discussing the boys on the field, the gossip around the sorority house, and the next dance.

The Baron's team got three runs in their first at bat, and dread invaded my being. They had a lineup of football players, an all Mid-America Conference (MAC) hoopster, a couple of hardball stars, and strutted around like they were destined to win. The three runs did not dissuade their confidence. But "hope springs eternal in the human breast," and by the end of the first inning we were only down a run. For five more innings it was back and forth, with lots of hits and lots of runs piling up. Actually the rising water floated all boats, and competition became a commonality between both sides, with respect being engendered with each change of the lead. In fact, the trappings of uniforms, or lack thereof, the competing wardrobes and smells of the bleachers and the obvious differences melted away in the heat of the action.

This was a softball game. Now, nothing else mattered, and winning was everything. We lead by a narrow one run with their top of the line-up batting in the bottom of the last inning. Three outs from glory and I could feel it, but only fleetingly. Two base hits and first and second occupied with no outs, Mr. All-MAC strolled cockily to the plate. All kind of rationalizations buzzed through my head: "Well, we made it this far, nothing to be ashamed of. We played some fine softball. It was fun anyway." All such nonsense losers recant to salve the pain of imminent defeat.

Mr. "Big Shot" scoured a scorching line drive between Paul and Skip, a sure hit with runners advancing. Depending on the throw from left field, the runner may or may not score, but the bases would still be loaded with no outs. All of a sudden, Skip leaped out of thin air angling toward the left field corner and in a full-out stretch, laid vertically in mid air, got his glove between the ball and the ground just before impact, and nestled the ball safely in its web. In an instant, all on practiced instinct, Skip bounced up and turned to fire the ball to second to double off the runner. Like stunned statues the infield stood, so second base was uncovered. Skip waved his arm at Lou to cover, and as if waking up from a Rip Van Winkle nap, Lou stumbled toward second base as Chip lobbed a soft toss to perfectly connect with Lou and beat the runner to the bag. Two outs, a man on first, and their power hitter strided to the plate. It was anybody's ball game now.

Little Joe lobbed a high back spin and it caught the outside of the plate for a called strike one. The next pitch was a little inside and Mr. Too-Big-for-His-Britches stepped toward third and cannoned one to left field. I knew instantly it would clear the fence by 100 feet. But inside balls are hard to hit straight and this one curved foul, by about 30 feet. One batter, one pitcher, one runner on base, one strike left, one out to go, one on one. It was not dread I felt, but another type of pure feeling that comes with the excited unknown of competing. It is not elation, not fear, not stomach-clenching sickness, but something more precious, pure and chaste and real and sublime known by those who love competition. Feelings aside, the athlete's focus must be on his action on the next pitch. On your toes, ready to field a grounder, dive to catch a line drive, cover first on an infield hit, or play cutoff man for a play at home if hit deep to right field, focus man, this is no time for feelings. Little Joe seemed nervous, not unusual, but all he had to do was get it over the plate and trust his field, for in slow-pitch softball, unlike in hardball, the pitcher is only a convenient ball delivery mechanism for hitters rather than a mano-a-mano feat of skill with sliders, fast balls, curves, change-ups, knuckle balls, and other such sundry choices pitchers use to thwart batters. So don't fret Little Joe, just give 'em your best pitch and toss fate to the gods of the diamond and your defense.

Oh my God, I didn't expect such a fat pitch, though. Right before his last pitch of the day reached the plate, I saw home run written between all the seams, and now I just didn't want it to end this way. But the gods tricked us all, and in one mighty swing, a monster stroke of the bat, a rotation with over-the-fences embedded in the very act, our Mr. Cool Guy tried to kill it, the kiss of death in baseball, golf, and sometimes hunting.

The ball snuck by and softly resided in Mike's glove.

"Strike three," the umpire shouted.

One more game and the Varmits could win their first official softball tournament. Smalley came in to pitch, but everything seemed a little anti-climactic to beating the Baron's team, and we won going away. The stands were full, mostly of eliminated teams curious to see if we were real or not. Some found themselves cheering for us, and after the win, many came up to shake our hands and congratulate us. Strike one up for the glories of sport, making flat the playing field of life, valuing the effort not the background, honoring those who came to play not for what they looked like, not for what they believed, but for how they played the game. Butt, butt, buddies dominated the jubilation and the camaraderie that comes with winning communicated loudly in looks, hand slaps, mutual pointing, and handshakes. The Varmits were on the softball map of Southeast Ohio and the Ohio Valley. Winning carries its own reward and satisfaction, and changes who people are and how they relate to one another, and my ties to Meigs County became forever and inextricably woven into the fabric of my being after that softball tournament, for I was a Varmit, at that time and forever, and proud of it.

Chapter 8: Neighborly Love, Corn, and Cream

Back at the farm there was lots to do. I built some stairs out of 10" x 10" x 3' rectangular rocks to abate a muddy slope on the walk from the parking lot to the house. Going it alone, macho-like, digging the shelf for them to rest upon, rolling and lifting the stones in place, filling dirt around them neatly, upon reflection, was the task that forever set my back back to the earlier days of humankind when humanoids did not walk upright, because for a few days that was what my stance resembled. The steps worked, my back didn't, but youth and aspirin slowly healed the pain.

As a reward, I headed out to the chicken coop across the lawn to gather some eggs from the layers left by Mickey and Anise. Replacing the usual squawking was an eerie silence, so surprising that even hunched over back pain didn't stop me from standing up a little and take notice. I cautiously opened the coop door and my premonition became a reality. Two chickens were missing and only blood and feathers remained on the hardened hay and chicken-shit floor while the rest of the brood looked on with fear in their eyes and hesitation in their bodies. A varmint of the four-legged variety had violated Scoop's coop.

"I'll kill the mother-fucker, or whatever it is," I thought.

"Any of you girls know anything about this massacre?" I pleaded to my fair-feathered friends. No answer. They had been sworn to secrecy by the most dastardly of villains.

I walked the perimeter of the coop looking for entry ways and found that on the back side opposite from the house a critter had dug a hole big enough to crawl into the coop and lay waste to a pair of sweet little layers.

I went back to the shed to retrieve a piece of ply board and some tools, and only minutes later the hole had a patch to challenge the most aggressive of predators. Figuring out the law of the jungle, or country as this might be, I knew that free food and live prey would entice my now archenemy to return in the near future.

Cathy, a colleague in Dr. W's class and a blue-collar raised sweetheart from Buffalo who started her graduate program with me a year earlier, came out the next day for sun, garden eats, and a get-a-way from school, her roommates, and other pressures of student life and to wander around the place in her panties in full daylight. Cathy had enormous breasts that even two cats, one dog, five geese, and I could not help but notice. She was sweet beyond candy, and although I surmised at times fond of me, was always a friend and good sport. Too much sun on white breasts was not a good combination, and for days, poor Cathy suffered the pain of sunburn and blisters in a very sensitive area.

As evening would fade, we'd sit in the lawn chairs by the root cellar talking and complaining about Dr. W. At dusk with the sky still holding onto the remains of the light of the day, but with darkened forest surrounding The Country Place, the magic light show commenced. Picture, gazing east away from the house, the slopping ground past the chicken coop with the forest and hill behind, and the slightly lighted sky above. In that dark swath of woods, the lightning bugs would dance. Their phosphorus lanterns flickered randomly against the dark.

Somewhere in my childhood the notion became part of my memory that lightning bugs, as we called them in Oklahoma, held magical powers. Dad and I caught one and put him (or her or it?) in a jar to observe up close. The tail would blink on and off frequently, mesmerizing a young man's gaze. The next morning I rushed to retrieve the jar from the front porch and took it into a dark bathroom to continue my fascination with the magic light show. Nothing. I shook the jar and still nothing. Slowly I carried the jar to Daddy and held it up to him, silent. He must have read my face and calmly took the jar and opened it. Turning it upside down he shook the contents into his large hand and fished around for the little bug.

"Here it is," he said. "I don't think it lived through the night." He placed the little black bug in my hand, and I stared at it wondering where the light was, had been, and whether or not it would flicker ever again.

My lower lip began to tremble, and somehow the notion of death and how pleasure is fleeting and fragile, became inextricably woven into my psyche that day. I would never catch another bug again.

So with memories of childhood, and a sense of the pure childlike joy and exhilaration of the magical natural power of the world around us, I tapped Cathy's beer and toasted to our friendship and the country, both special in my heart. But the memory of the moment is forever pierced by what happened next: "Holy shit, there's that sonofabitch down there!"

Cathy nearly dropped her beer in her ample cleavage. I jumped up and raced down the hill toward the pen, flailing my arms, yelling like a mad man, and readying myself for a man vs. beast encounter. At about twenty feet, a startled dog, not more than a pup, raced off through the woods, bounded across the creek, and hightailed it out of sight. It was a reddish mutt, Irish Setter-looking, but sure to have had other breeds in its breeding line to look like that. With hands on my hips, I hollered into the dying of the light, "You fucking egg-sucking and chicken-killing dog!"

Dogs are different than other animals that live on death, killing and the meat of the hunt. It is practical for wolves, tigers, lions, hyenas, and other feared predators of the night to eat what they kill, and they rarely, if ever, kill for sport. Dogs, even sweet, cute, domesticated, fluffy, little pet-type ones, when falling into a pack of others, will taste a little blood and kill indiscriminately, wantonly, and continuously. It is carnage way beyond hunger. What I had here was a dog that loved eggs, had figured out that chickens are fair game, and had wandered back to the scene of his (or her) previous transgressions. This predator could not catch a rooster, for just as the dog thought he had something to sink his teeth into, the rooster had just enough sense and wings to fly up and out of reach. The laying hens were not so lucky: in the pen popping out eggs daily, they were sitting ducks, so to speak.

The next day I wandered across the road and asked Little Joe if he knew who had a red dog around here. "That'd be Red, down the road a piece," he said pointing south toward the Union Baptist Church. So a Red fellow has a red dog. OK, there's symmetry. I decided to walk that way to collect my thoughts about how to approach a guy I'd never met and what to say to him about his dog killing my chickens. Sure enough, just as Little Joe had described, about half a mile or so down the road was what must have been Red's house. Without the farm equipment scattered around the yard, all of which looked to be in good repair and ready for field action, the house could have been viewed as abandoned. Paint had not blessed the boards for decades, so the walls had a natural weathered look bordering on rotten. North of the house was a long, low shed full of more farm equipment, bales of hay, an old car or two, and a dog house.

With a deep breath and confident stride, I waded amongst the weeds in the front, checked the first porch step for firmness, and slowly walked up and knocked on the door.

Nothing. Silence. I paused and knocked louder. Warm kitchen smells of baking bread faintly wafted around the house, so I surmised someone was home, hopefully not readying a shot gun to be rid of the intruder. One more knock and a farm woman slowly opened the door as she wiped her hands with a kitchen towel. She said nothing.

"Pardon me, Ma'am, but I'm kinda your neighbor and I was wondering if Red is here, I need to talk with him," I said.

"Let me git him," she said.

Red came to the door and said come on in. He was a slight man, into his seventies I surmised, with stooped shoulders, bowed legs, and greasy hair. He stuck out his hand and said, "I'm Red Buzzard."

Could this be real? I did want to, given that his name was Red Buzzard, say I was Rocky Raccoon, Harry Black Hawk, Blue Bird, but I just politely said, "Mine's Ted."

He offered me a seat and, before my butt hit the cushion, I began my story of where I live, having seen a reddish dog around my chicken coop, missing lots of eggs and two layers dead as a barn door, etc.

"Whatcha say about a farm whore?" he quizzed. "I'm a little hard of hearing. Speak up, young man," he said.

"I LIVE ONE FARM OVER AND A RED DOG HAS BEEN KILLING MY CHICKENS. DO YOU HAVE A RED DOG?" I yelled. Now I was good at this, for my granddaddy became increasingly hard of hearing in his eighties and was pretty hearing-impaired when he moved in with us to live out his last days. He brought with him a horn on a cord with an ear piece and I'd holler into that small megaphone attached to the flexible cord with the other end in Granddaddy's ear. It worked for a while, until the calcium deposits on his head drove him crazy, or so he thought.

"Do I have a red hog?" he questioned.

"NO, A RED DOG." I upped the volume and he nodded.

"Yep, we got a new one around here somewhere," he knowingly stated.

So I told him the story in jaw-rattling decibels, asking what I should do about his dog eating my eggs and killing my chickens. There was a very long pause. I just know this farmer has some tricks up his sleeves, for he had lived a long life on the farm, and old sages like this just know this kind of shit. A creative solution was brewing in his brain.

With incredulous simplicity, tones of matter-of-factness, and why are you asking me such a silly question in his voice, he boldly declared, "Well, shoot the sonofabitch!!!"

Not what I had anticipated, but what I would learn is the way of the farm. There are animals for livelihood and animals for recreation and companionship, although some do perform worthwhile tasks and stunts of endearment, but the law of the land is protect your money by whatever means necessary. Dogs that kill chickens give up any right to life on a farm. I never saw that dog again. Several days later I found a box in the corner of the coop with a couple of mid-size chicks waddling around happily. They grew to be fine layers. Every once in a while I'd take a dozen eggs and put them in the old and weathered milk box on the porch of Red and his wife. I only saw Red one other time after that. But human bonding manifests itself in strange ways, and I always felt that Red was my friend.

Later, I heard of a neighbor shooting an old dog of Red's years before my association with him. Red got pissed off and went over to this guy's house and shot one of his cows. The sheriff came and questioned Red about the shooting.

"He shot my dog," Red replied.

The sheriff asked again thinking Red did not hear him.

"He shot my dog," Red said more emphatically.

Red never heard from the sheriff again. So country retribution trumped farm animal vs. expendable pet values.

It was party weekend. OK, most every weekend was party weekend at The Country Place, but Greg's college quasi-girlfriend was coming to visit and it was time to light up the BBQ, listen to a little Willie, and talk Texan. I knew Leigh at TCU; she dormed with several of my girlfriends, we went to parties together, and a few times we double-dated when she and Greg and whomever and I was with would go to the movies. She was a real red-headed Texas type gal; shy, quiet, smart, but shy and quiet, if I failed to mention that.

Hip was rolling joints, Captain Crunch was picking garden vegetables with Leigh, I was cooking up a storm in the kitchen, and Roberta Flack was crooning "Feel Like Makin' Love" on the stereo. It was a TCU reunion, transplanted to the hills of Ohio. BBQ, green beans with bacon, some coleslaw, corn on the cob, and a fresh pecan pie in the oven meant life was good on the farm, thanks Mr. Denver. There's an art to fresh-corn picking, cooking, and eating. Lots of folks will tell you how they do it, corn things that is, but real connoisseurs of all things corn should follow our procedures. Put a pot of water on the stove so it boils just before sitting down to supper, and just as you serve up the other dishes, go out to the garden with another person carrying the pot of water. Quickly shuck a few ears of ripe corn, fully developed, tassels dark and draped, and plop them in the water. When you get back in the house serve up the corn immediately with those little corn holders stuck in the side. Never try to butter corn with a knife, that shit don't work. Holding the corn holders, just run the corn catawampus (a word common to my upbringing that meant "crosswise" or "out of line" but one I have no earthly idea how to spell) across a stick of butter creating a nice little corn-size well in the butter for others to use. Now for the controversial part: some use salt, some do not. Some use pepper, some do not. Some use both, some do not. Personally, I'm a salt alone man, for pepper hides the kernel's sweetness while salt heightens the candy aspect of each little morsel. Hip and I set the record for ears eaten in one setting, ten each, and we're damn proud of it. Now others will advocate for high-heat roasting on the grill with shucks almost burnt to really enjoy corn. Whatever. Why hell, I always put *a bean* in my chili so as to not be a hard-ass purist in the kitchen of opinions.

Corn, known now throughout the world, was originally a New World find when Columbus and other sailor daredevils of yesteryear failed to find the Far East and "discovered" the Americas, without a nod to all kinds of Indians who lived here and felt they belonged to this earth. But they gave us corn. My family had a little Choctaw in our heritage, so "us" has always been ambiguous to me.

Corn, a grass with goodies. From stalk, to tassel, kernels to blades, silks to husks, stems to flowers, seeds to roots, corn stands tall in its field. For thousands of years, originating from the grass called *teosinte*, cultivated into hundreds of different varieties, a staff of life staple on the dinner plate of many cultures, glorified in rock art, jewelry, sand paintings, trinkets, amulets, and garments of celebration and war. Corn, originally *mahiz*, amazing maize. Corn, requiring the natives to wander less and cultivate more, changed the nomadic and eating habits of generations and millions of peoples throughout the Americas. Sweet, dent, flint, popcorn, flour, waxy, pod, corn of many species, used in filler for plastics, packing/insulating materials, adhesives, chemicals, explosives, paint, paste, abrasives, dyes, insecticides, pharmaceuticals, organic acids, solvents, rayon, antifreeze, soaps, and many more things. Corn, the munificent vegetable: can it, cream it, mush it for babies, dry it, roast it, pop it, grind it into grits, eat it on the cob, cut it off and spoon it into your mouth. Corn, star of harvest ceremonies, only cultivated for humankind, not growing wild for thousands of years. One of the three sisters with beans and squash, culinary cornerstone of the Aztecs, Incas, Mayas, Pueblo, Pawtuxet Indians, and a whole lot of others. The phallic fruit, average rows of sixteen, always even, about 800 kernels per ear, one piece of silk for every kernel, and grown from southern North Dakota to southern Argentina and Peru, from New England to the watershed of the Colorado River, and most places in between. Corn is king! Make it into puddings, tamales, tortillas, succotash, and soups. Cook up some cornbread and call it Johnny Cakes or hoe cakes, distill it into spirits, mash and ferment it into beer. Ancients created corn husk bed mats, clothing, moccasins, cornhusk dolls, tote bags, and told stories about how the gift of the deities was delivered by the crow and planted from the Corn Grandmother whose blood spread around the field yielded rows of life-giving food. Big time livestock feed, supplier of corn oil, ethanol, starch, sugar, glucose, dextrose, and the ever-controversial high-fructose corn syrup (HFCS), regal yet derided, source of greed while fattening folks, worshipped yet denigrated. It's even used in Candy Corn, which only looks like corn, sorta. Corn, involved in grisly human sacrifice and the nutritional salvation to hundreds of millions not sacrificed. Corn, found in 3000 grocery items, including glue, shoe polish, aspirin, ink, marshmallows, ice cream, and cosmetics. Make a corncob pipe and smoke up some wacky tobacco, for it's the official grain of Wisconsin, while Nebraska is the Cornhusker State, and there is a famous Corn Palace in Mitchell, South Dakota. Measure it by the bushel, weighing 56 pounds, squeeze 33 pounds of sweetener, 32 pounds of starch, and 2.5 gallons of ethanol out of a bushel, but maybe this is all a little corny.

Drinking and smoking long into the evening had us all a little tired, so Hip went off to read and Greg fell asleep in the rocker. His snoring got louder as Leigh and I sat on the couch quietly talking. One-on-one, she transformed from wall-flower to sweet conversationalist, engaging, humorous, and oh so sweet. I ask how it goes with ol' Captain Crunch and she airs her frustration straightforwardly, indicating what I had always known, that being in relationship with Greg, from a women's perspective, was not a satisfying event. Shirley, a previous girlfriend of his, would bend my ear for hours venting her issues with her man. This was déjà vu all over again. With empathy I nodded, understanding. The next actual pieces of conversation fade about here. All I remember is two people, quite quietly and conspiratorially, like little kids sneaking out of the kitchen after raiding the off-limits cookie jar, closing the upstairs door behind us and tip-toeing to the loft of love.

Leigh had ivory skin, more white than white, a long neck, wonderfully swaying breasts, a narrow waist, baby-making hips, and oh yes, she was definitely a natural red-haired lass, for tucked between her legs protecting the lips of love was a tuft of the softest red hair one's nose could encounter. Luckily, lovemaking pounds the heart more than the fear of being discovered. She dressed slowly in the moonlight, I had no idea what had just happened, but a smile came to my face as I kissed her cheek goodbye and she slipped down the stairs and told Greg she was going to bed and to not disturb her. He mumbled something and fell back to sleep tilted in the rocker at a weird angle.

I was left there in the attic alone with strains of Rusty Weir's song playing in my head. He premiered that song one evening in a lounge in Austin, Texas with his friend and wife in attendance, and as a surprise spoof, to the absolute shock of both, belted out these lines looking right at his friend: "Well it's around the town that you've been seeing (my wife), and I called you up to ask if it were true. I heard you been laying my old lady . . ."

Leigh later left to go home to Texas. She left Greg and left me a wink. She is still a love in my life. She lives alone, finding it easier to put up with a lot of cats that terrorize her abode than a man that does not meet her standards.

The next day, a sunny Sunday, I did what any self-respecting Okie would do: went for a drive in the country to visit friends. Bob had invited me to his farm to buy some milk out of his "milker" cow if I wanted some. Now this was right up my alley, or farm lane. Back in the good ol' days in our very suburban home in OKC, my dad would ever so often go just a mile or so over to Mr. Fisher's place and purchase a gallon or two of raw milk. He'd let it settle and with me watching, carefully skim off the cream that settles to the top of the gallon jar with a ladle. He'd talk about how they had a separator back on the farm in Northwest Oklahoma when he was a boy. Why cream that is called "heavy cream" is lighter than milk and floats to the top has always been a conundrum to me. Mom would whip us some cream with a little sugar and vanilla to top off one of her pies, Daddy would use the cream in his coffee, and us kids would down the milk like water.

WW, a good ol' girl fellow grad student from Buffalo, was visiting The Country Place that day. WW stood for Wrong Way, a nickname tribute appropriately tagged on her when she got us terminally lost in the hills of West Virginia on a white water expedition. So with her and Hip loaded in the old maroon Impala we all turned south by the little store and wandered through the hills of Meigs County, turned up a little rise and a drive. I knew I'd found the right place when "Scoop, Scoop" pierced the tranquility of the pastoral setting. Bob lived with Mr. "Butt butt, buddy" himself, Smalley, and his chick, French Fry. The old house made Red's place look like a proverbial mansion in the Hamptons. Vertical house boards just did not come together, right angles weren't plentiful. Why, this was the finder's paradise for barn wood picture frames, for that is all I could think of that this shack of shit could be purposely used. A big old barn, actually in better condition, loomed large near the house. Cornfields stretched into the distance, farm implements lay waiting around the yard, and dogs, chickens, cats, and other mangy critters loped around everything.

Bob shook hands with WW, said "Hi" to Hip, and motioned us inside. It was not the Taj Mahal. Stuffing popped out of old couches, shredded rugs barely protected the floor, kitchen cabinets were scattered with an assortment of farm and cooking things, drug paraphernalia, food stuff, and bottling supplies. There was a big telephone line spool, four feet across, acting as a coffee table, or rather a joint-rolling station. Bob waded through the clutter, opened up an old porcelain fridge, and hauled out a couple of gallons of milk, leaving countless others in their cool abode. Dollars were passed, and Bob asked us if we wanted to see his cornfield. "Sure," I responded. The others nodded.

Now this was no ordinary cornfield. About every fourth stalk grew a bushier plant that had no tassels, no forming corn, and no long, sharp leaves. These plants had fanned hands of jagged, narrow leaves, and not being stupid, I commented on the nice crop. *High Times* magazine was a staple around The Country Place and contained countless pictures of some fine marijuana groves, so I knew what this was, although these were the first actual plants I had the privilege to meet in the raw. Hip, who was much more experienced in all things marijuana, stood there in utter awe.

"This is a lot of shit," I exclaimed, realizing once again that it is the mark of a genius one who can state the obvious. Proudly, Bob agreed. This is the moment I knew I was no longer just a softball teammate that lived on the Ridge. This was the moment that trust superseded just knowing one another, when information was shared, information that, if not held in confidence, could send your friend to jail, or tip scoundrels to rip off the crop. Uncontrolled words that get around can be detrimental to one's health, livelihood, and well-being. I had passed the milk test. Even more astounding, Bob trusted my friends as well. Before me lay hundreds of dope plants, not quite ripe, buds not fully-formed, THC still making its way from soil to stem, given hot sun and cool water. Bob assured me that we'd have some left over to smoke all winter and we headed back with our booty of cream and milk to cook up some dinner.

That evening I ritualistically skimmed the cream off the top just like Daddy used to do and put some in a quart jar in the fridge. Filling another quart jar about a quarter up, I summoned the boys of The Country Place and WW. I asked them if they knew what I had in my hand.

"Yea, cream, man," Hip sarcastically stated.

"No, man," I intoned back. "This is butter."

"Doesn't look like any butter I've ever seen," Greg said.

At which moment I began vigorously to shake the jar like an automatic paint mixer. With teeth gritted, and muscles rippling, I was dancing, shaking, and jiving around the room to the boogie-woogie beat of the Doobie Brothers' "Listen to the Music" with my hand cradling the jar and my arm whipping back and forth like beating the meat, whipping the devil, shaking a milky dew drop off a red nose on a blue veiner, a practiced motion, with plenty of muscle memory to get the job done.

"Oh my god, It's coming . . . together," I orgasmically screamed. WW was hysterical. The remaining goo in the jar was light yellow, and solidified with only a tablespoon of almost clear milky liquid remaining around the stuff in the jar. With a dramatic twist of the cap and a Shakespearean stage gesture of flair using a spatula, I scooped out the light yellowish substance from the jar and molded it into a little cup, mixing a little salt as I proceeded.

"Voila." I madly exclaimed. "Pass me a cracker, we have butter to try."

Ain't nothing like fresh butter, whole cream, rich milk, and the ensuing products they can create. Life was good, the garden bountiful, the chickens happy, Cranfield rewarded with his food embellished with the liquid residuals from the butter "churn" jar, the cats sleeping non-fazed in the living room, rock and roll music pulsating around us, and a fine joint of Meigs County's finest making the rounds, all I could think was, thanks to John Denver, "Thank God I'm a country boy!"

Chapter 9: The Crook Resigns

"Therefore, I shall resign the Presidency effective at noon tomorrow. Vice President Ford will be sworn in as President at that hour in this office."
(Richard Nixon, August 8, 1974)

It's a toss-up whether to celebrate happy trails to ol' Tricky Dick on the eighth or ninth of August, but the Nixon resignation was such a watershed and historical event in American history, and so significant for the rule of law, that we just might need two days to cheer, drink strong grog, dance, and generally revel in the hope that democracy has a fighting chance. Being a graduate student is a self-absorptive time in one's life, but not all the focus is on learning and earning. Not only are there grades, papers due, and classes to prepare for, there is also, of course, beer to drink, girls to fondle, dope to smoke, and porn movies to watch. So it was an ebb in the flow of personal political involvement during my Athens days that found me more apolitical than usual. But even in my state of political apathy, I was not one to ignore the first time a sitting President of these great United States would resign under duress and disgrace. The apolitical part was certainly not always the case in my life, quite the contrary.

I ran for office from the earliest of times: President of the 6th grade class, Student Council officer in high school, student leader in several organizations in college. My college freshman roommate was a debater from Edmond, Oklahoma. In fact, the previous year he had won the National Forensic League high school debate championship. The debate topic our freshman year was something like, "Resolved that the U.S. government should substantially reduce its foreign policy commitments." That, of course, centered on the argument of getting out of Vietnam or staying the course. Brad had stacks and stacks of evidentiary material, and I read everything that he carried into the room including the Gulf of Tonkin Resolution in its entirety. After long discussions, his permeated with the rational honing of a world-class debater, mine righteously indignant social injustice diatribes, we decided it was time to act. So that springtime of 1967, Brad and I joined a group that was "picketing" against the war on the front steps of the Federal Building in downtown Ft. Worth, protesting our involvement in a morally, politically, militarily, and economically disastrous and misguided venture. That's when I got a file. The "Federales" came out and filmed the whole event, at least us "radicals." I don't know if they turned the cameras toward those proud American citizens who drove by in their shiny pick-up trucks yelling sweet nothings to us while holding up a finger that must have meant we were number one.

"Commie, fascist pig" was common, but "hippie son-of-a-bitch" in a Texas accent worked pretty well, too. I earned my anti-Vietnam credentials early.

A few years later, I was the key organizer at TCU's protest of the Kent State massacre. Later in the spring of 1970, Keith and I organized a TCU version of a national movement on college campuses against the war. We read the names of the war dead from the front steps of the Brown Lupton Student Center. We organized a rally around the "Frog Fountain," a ridiculous above-ground eyesore with mushroom-shaped copper towers that spewed water everywhere in the Texas wind. Perhaps the most significant accomplishment of the spring was convincing the Faculty Senate to declare a special day when all classes would discuss the war as it related to the subject of the class. I wanted to sit in an ROTC class to hear how the military instructors would approach the subject, but they would not let me.

After graduation, I worked one summer as the only white male member on an African-American theatre troupe doing theatre on the back of a flatbed truck trailer in predominately black neighborhoods around Ft. Worth and Dallas. The program was funded by some offshoot of legislation passed during the Johnson Administration to abate summer riots in large cities across America. I met a bunch of wonderful people and learned to speak inner-city Black. Luckily I lived to tell about the hot Texas evening when a young black man standing two feet away got shot in the stomach. Luckily he lived to tell about it as well. Just know it is exponentially different to hear a gun shot at close range and watch a friend fall in agony in person than to see it on TV crime and western shows.

Social activism, political involvement, and issues of justice were all inextricably woven into the fabric of my life, so Nixon's resignation did not go unnoticed. Earlier in the 1970s, I had served as a counselor at a Unitarian summer camp in Forked River, NJ, with my friend Harold, a self-proclaimed "wandering Jewnitarian." Our friendship I confess, was a bit taxed by the fact his previous summer's girlfriend switched mates to me for the current summer. Each night the lovely and young Kate and I would help get the campers snuggled in their beds, and then sneak into the director's apartment, where the camp's only TV resided. It was a small old black-and-white set bordering on antique status even then, but through the fuzz we watched the late night reruns of the Watergate Hearings in full detail. We were mesmerized, spellbound, captured, and hooked on the greatest reality show of all time. The firing of Cox, the release of the tapes with missing sections, Dean's confession, the Senate hearings, all before us in shades of gray on the tiny TV in that tiny room.

In any case, it looked like a typical church camp, complete with a mess hall, a baseball diamond, tennis courts, rustic cabins, and an old church. It was located on the grounds where the Universalists and Unitarian leaders forged a not-so-perfect union. So I remember the Watergate news and hearings precisely, watching TV so closely and fondly, more because of what happened when the TV went off. By then, hot and horny as hell, Kate and I would slip away to my cozy dorm room for outrageous sexual escapades, made all the more exciting because such clandestine romps were sorely frowned upon by the director. All this led Kate and me to give meaningful nuance to the moniker "Tricky Dick." For the next thirty years, whenever the topic of Watergate would arise in conversation my ol' tricky dick would as well. Ah, memories abide.

In 1974 the events Kate and I had watched so closely in the camp finally led to Nixon's resignation. By then, I was in Ohio hanging out in the country with beer-swigging and dope-smoking hippies.

With strains of Olivia Newton-John breathily filling The Country Place from the little turntable, we toasted a cold Rolling Rock to a transition in the pages of American History as Air Force One flew west to deposit the deposed to be a forever non-powerful footnote secluded behind the walls of his San Clemente compound.

"Did you know that Olivia is Female Vocalist of the Year?" Hip stated after a long drag on a plus-sized doobie.

"No, but I think she's sexy, kinda like Marilyn Chambers, you know, the Ivory Snow model," I said.

How we got our news of the day out in the country always surprised me. We were TV-less and no newspaper graced our door each morning. When I drove between home and Athens the radio was mostly music, and when at the university, it was classes and books. *The Post*, an admirable student newspaper, published some national and international news in summary form, but not in depth. So I was not always up to speed on the trial of Patricia Hearst, the nineteen-year-old granddaughter of William Randolph Hearst, charged with robbing a bank in San Francisco in April with the Symbionese Liberation Army. Unrelated but somehow cosmically linked, Hiroo Onoda, a Second Lieutenant in the Japanese Army in World War II, finally decided to surrender in the Philippines. Wow, who was he fighting all those years? Don't think he got a newspaper either. Commended or ridiculed, let's face it, "never give up" never had a more ardent follower.

1974 was a hell of a year. Chet Huntley died symbolizing the end of news we could trust. The economy sucked as inflation reached 11%, so it was a great time to be in school. We faced an oil embargo crisis and the subsequent nationwide implementation of the 55 mph speed limit (unless you drove a Cadillac in Texas). Thanks to the energy crisis at least we got Daylight Saving Time four months early so we could have more summer light for late evening dips in the pond.

The years between 1967 and 1974 had done a lot to dash the hopes of a generation that believed with JFK that we should "Ask not what your country can do for you, but what you can do for your country." We survived his assassination, but it became harder to take when Martin Luther King, Jr. and Bobby Kennedy fell. The establishment we felt had taken us to war, trashed the economy, illegally wiretapped, lied about it, sent dope smokers to jail, and killed Negros in the South. The Soviet Union expelled Aleksandr Solzhenitsyn while still pointing weapons of mass destruction at every major city in America, but not thank God, little Meigs County, Appalachian hill country the world had seemingly forgot.

Ah, but "hope springs eternal in the human breast," for in April a black man swatted his 715th home run over the left field wall at Atlanta-Fulton County Stadium, making the Brave's Hank Aaron the all-time home run hitter and bringing unwanted fame to LA Dodgers pitcher Al Downing. The fan-aided romp around the bases probably fried the chicken-fried racist crowd below the Mason-Dixon Line. Take that, you crackers!

In another stunning feat of physical prowess, French acrobat Philippe Petit walked across a high wire strung across the sky between the World Trade Towers to the shock and amazement of New Yorkers gawking skyward in disbelief. He gave all us anti-establishment and anti-authoritarians great hope that the system of powers could be fooled, challenged, and dazzled.

Yes, that June more was happening in the world than Varmit softball in Southeast Ohio. Why, just up the road in Troy, a pack of Wrigley Chewing gum was imprinted with the first Universal Product Code and was "scanned" at a cash register. Also up the road a piece, the Cleveland Indians hosted "Ten Cent Beer Night," but had to forfeit the game to the Texas Rangers due to drunken and unruly fans, something the Aussies would never let happen in a Cricket Test. Charles Lindbergh, Tex Ritter, Agnes Moorehead, Duke Ellington, Mama Cass Elliott, Ed Sullivan, Jack Benny, and Juan Peron died. To take their places, Derek Jeter, Jewel, Leonardo DiCaprio, Hilary Swank, and Penelope Cruz were all born.

None of this did I actually know at the time, oh, except ol' Tex and maybe The Spirit of St. Louis guy. I had a garden to tend, classes to attend, and females to please, so my attention was not on the news or history of the day. I was picking a few tomatoes in the garden one afternoon when Valerie came walking up the hill with her baby and asked if she might take a swim in the pond.

"Sure," I replied. "The fish will nibble your toes."

As she walked up the hill I strolled along for company and to pick some cattails for a salad. Being a regular Euell Gibbons-type, the naturalist that stalked the earth for wild, edible things and wrote cookbooks, I had just learned that the roots of the cattails were quite tasty, a little like water chestnuts. Valerie stripped herself naked, tossed little Stephanie's diaper on the ground and slid into the water with baby held tightly to her breast. Although well into her twenties, Valerie appeared as if she had just reached puberty. Her childlike body held innocence and immaturity and unconscious sexiness. Naked bodies and babies emit sensuality, so I decided to cool off with my pond mates.

"What are you picking up here?" she asked.

"Oh, some cattails to put in a salad," I responded. "They are pretty good—the Indians used to eat them a lot. Early settlers called them nature's supermarket, or at least their word for that concept." Feeling quite erudite and having just read about these water-loving plants, I continued. "The young cattail stalk is also known as "cossack asparagus" and the immature flower, the kitten tail, were eaten as vegetables. The pollen and root were used to make flour for baking and cooking. The stalks and leaves were used for making rope, baskets, shelter, bedding, and clothing. The cottony seed head was used for stuffing bedding and baby diapers," I noted as I gestured to the one on the ground not far from me, "and the cigar-shaped catkin was dipped in animal fat and used as a torch."

I was on a roll. I'm not sure if Valerie was impressed, stunned, or bored, but at least she was attentive.

"That's not all though: cattails act as nature's water filters. They provide a cleaning service, filtering toxins from the water in which they grow. They also provide a valuable wildlife habitat, used for cover, roosting, nesting, and food."

Ending my ethnobotany lecture, I helped Valerie out of the pond and held Stephanie while I watched her dress. I had never held a wet and naked baby. She was so small, light, warm, and soft and she was cooing sweetly. As I looked into her eyes, and she looked at me, I was entranced. Something inside me, instinct, nature, myth, genes, hormones, psyche, or some other deep-seated human emotion momentarily mesmerized me. I hesitantly handed the baby back to Valerie. I put on my jeans and T-shirt, picked up my gatherings, and we walked down the hill together. Valerie thanked me and headed home. As she walked away, I paused there reflecting upon my future place in a family and my role someday as a father. "When might it happen," I pondered, "and with whom?" But politics, social justice, fatherhood, babies, school, and the future would just have to wait. For on that evening I had a party to get to in Athens. So I put on my cowboy boots, plopped the Stetson on my head, mounted my old maroon Chevy, and rode into town, tipping my hat to the Catawba tree with a well-accented Texas drawl: "Howdy and seeyalader."

Chapter 10: Perfect Company and The Ball Mason Perfect Company

It's a Buck Dancers Choice, my friend,
better take my advice
You know all the rules by now
and the fire from the ice
Will you come with me?
Won't you come with me?
Whoa-oh what I want to know,
will you come with me?

It's the same story the crow told me
It's the only one he know—
like the morning sun you come
and like the wind you go
Ain't no time to hate,
barely time to wait
Whoa-oh, what I want to know,
where does the time go?
(Robert Hunter and Jerry Garcia, "Uncle John's Band")

At Cathy's house not far from campus, lots of grad students were hanging out drinking beer, swapping academic horror stories, bemoaning the workload, and toking on some joints. She had told me to come by after studying so there I was, not one to miss free beer or a party, especially one with women. As I entered the living room, Rich, a recent acquaintance, spotted me in the doorway and hollered out in a really bad Southern accent, "Boy, howyadoin'?" Now, Rich grew up very Italian in New York, and he thought us types from the plains lived in teepees, chased buffalo, and were generally uncultured. He loved to put on that really bad accent and give me a hard time. So I played along for his enjoyment. In a very loud and commanding voice, I yelled back at him feigning anger.

"Boy, you call me boy! Six foot three, 185 pounds of be-bopping, rip-roaring hell, a yard of dick, a bushel of balls, enough hair on my ass to weave an Indian blanket, and you call me BOY?" The place went dead silent. People did not know whether to shit or jump in the pot. Rich was staggered and overwhelmed, and he loved it. As the room remained silent, he sauntered over with a slight grin on his face. He picked me up and bear-hugged me and everyone hooted and hollered.

"Come on, I'll buy you a beer, Tex." (To those Northeastern, big-city boys, Texas and Oklahoma were pretty much the same. Just be real careful where and when you fail to make that distinction.)

I butterflied around the house drinking beer, picking up on conversations, psyching out the chicks, telling tall tales, and smoking weed. I drew a long toke, and handed the joint to Miriam, Cathy's roommate, whom I had met when I helped Cathy move into the house earlier that summer. Miriam was a tall, slender hippie chick in a free-flowing prairie dress with no bra. As hippie protocol dictated, she had unshaven legs and armpits, a faint mustache, and long stringy hair. Her half-masked eyes were the opposite of direction or aggression. They were eyes that flowed with the universe, eyes that were receptive and responsive without opinion, eyes that were not unfamiliar to pain and disappointment, eyes that even oh-so-watery and red from dope smoking, glanced my way and held my interest. We chatted using the surface of language, but the inner context of communication spoke loudly of hormones and body smells uncomplicated by perfume. We were beings aligning on another plain that went beyond mere spoken language. Oh yea, it also could have been a head full of cannabis, but I know cognitively after extensive research about interpersonal communication (excuse me, I was after all a graduate student in those studies) that little of our meaning is communicated via words, while most of the meaning we attribute to our communication comes from non-verbal cues, voice inflection, tone, and other non-word phenomena. As "strangers in a strange land," we "groked," à la author Robert A. Heinlein.

As normal, I waxed on about the joy of living in the country—the animals, my garden, good country cooking, the Varmits, the fireflies, the pond and the tranquility. Miriam did not say much (I've already asserted the unnecessary nature of words) but her eyes did speak, nod, affirm, confirm, respond, and give testament to blossoming carnal communication.

"I'd like to visit your country place some day," she softly spoke as she touched my arm and walked away holding her glance ever-so-subtly. As she glided back into the kitchen, my eyes saw an "earth momma." I envisioned her, banjo on lap, sitting on the porch swing of a dilapidated home in some hollow, playing "Foggy Mountain Breakdown," cooking biscuits, having babies, and raising pigs. It was not known whether it was a life chosen or not. It was getting late so I said my good-byes to Cathy and Rich, and drove off with the image of Miriam in my mind.

The next morning was my initiation into the world of country canning. Ball jars were a hot commodity in 1974, with all of America planting gardens, canning peaches, and trying to prepare for the imminent Armageddon. There was a big run on canning jars, lids, and rings—they were nowhere to be found. After futile forays into the stores of the area, with nary a canning jar in sight, I called the Ball Company in Muncie, Indiana, and asked to talk to an executive. I just told you canning jars were nowhere to be found on the shelves of retail America. Why, there was even a black market for used jars, and new ones were sold at scalpers' prices outside county Extension Service canning classes. It was a lack-of-commodity frenzy, a supply need of voluminous proportions. So I calmly discussed my dilemma with the Ball executive, telling him my heartfelt story of moving to the country, planting a garden, and wanting to can a lot of peaches. Maybe canning could help me find Jesus, I implied. He said that he doesn't get many requests from individuals for shipments of jars, but I responded that I thought he was the kind of guy who would understand, that he was a man of action, and he would be willing to help. Now, how could he resist? Maybe it was the fact that I volunteered to drive to Muncie and pick them up that convinced him of my sincerity. He offered to waive the shipping bill. So with a promise to send him a check for four cases of Ball canning jars, at wholesale prices I might add, it was only a few days before a note appeared in the mailbox that boxes awaited me at the main post office in Albany.

The old Coonfield motto was at work here: "If it's worth doing, it's worth overdoing." So with the promise of ninety-six jars to fill, I went to an Extension Service canning program to learn about how not to kill your friends with botulism or blow up the farmhouse with an over-agitated pressure cooker. My classmates had countless exchanges about how to acquire canning jars. I remained coy and evasive about my source, saying I inherited some from my great aunt, or something like that.

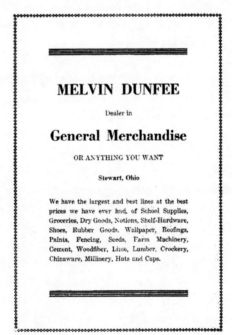

About this time, I was heading east out of Athens on a trip to somewhere with a vague tip from a friend about an old general store that time had forgotten. Sure enough, there along the highway I found the old place in Stewart, Ohio. "Melvin Dunfee, General Merchandise," the very faded sign across the door read. Even though it looked dark and closed, I pried open the old rickety wood frame screen door with a Wonder Bread push plate across the center, and walked into the 1920s, with hints of the 1940s thrown in for modernity. The emporium was dark, dank, and historical. A pickle barrel sat in the middle of the room with salt deposit rings around where the brine used to rise. The shelves looked as if they had not been tampered with in decades.

"Looking for something?" an old, quiet voice spoke out of the dark space. Following the sound, I tracked the source to an old man sitting behind the counter reading a paperback book. How he could read in such darkness was a mystery to me, but he and this old place seemed to hold other mysteries as well. I thought of glib replies, like, "An honest man," "my grandparents," or "parts for a Model T," but quietly decided that this was a guy who suffered no fools so I plainly replied: "Got any canning jars for sale?"

Slowly and laboriously he arose from his stool and came around the counter to check me out and point to the far corner of the store. There stood a wooden shelf full of stuff, much of which I had never seen. I did not have the foggiest notion what their contents held. But sure enough, there on the bottom shelf were a few cases of old canning jars, still in the original cardboard box, quite yellowed and tattered. I gently picked up a box with a corner peeling back from the staples, and pulled out a jar to observe and assess. OK, this was new to me. I held a blue glass jar, slightly bigger than a standard quart with tin lids lined on the inside with pearly white porcelain.

"Do these still work for canning?" I inquired skeptically.

After a long pause, he softly yet sarcastically said, "Well, I ain't dead yet, now am I?"

I guessed that meant yes.

"How much?" I asked.

"Oh, give me five bucks for the case." (It had twelve in it) That was less than I had paid for the new jars ordered from the Ball Company.

"Can you spare two cases?" I asked.

"Oh, I think my life will go on a little longer without 'em," he deadpanned.

Still holding the box sample in my hand, I noticed that the jar was a Ball Mason Perfect. "How perfect," I thought.

"You Melvin Dunfee?" I inquired.

"Last I checked," the old man replied.

The store would not let go of me. Amid spider webs and mouse droppings, every shelf, nook, and cranny, showcase and rack held products of ancient Americana. A few of the items I remembered from visits to my aunt and uncle's farm in Northwest Oklahoma. There were cases of Arm & Hammer Soda and Calumet Baking Powder. There was fishing gear, horse tack, feed, witch hazel jars, horehound candy, old water pump parts, and hardware from before my time. There were thousands of items, some beyond their usefulness, some as good as the day they were manufactured, and some just good old antiques. The smells of oil, lavender sachets, pickle barrel salt, rotting wood, tanned leather, cardboard, and grain magically tantalized my nostrils and prompted memories of begotten years of childhood that I don't vividly remember but surely experienced. It was a quiet orgasm of a high, supplanting the notion that drugs are needed for altered states of consciousness. I was just intoxicated by the past.

With the exchange of a ten spot and gracious thanks, I drove back to The Country Place armed and ready for canning all things of fruit and vegetable matter. Later, I would find an ad for Melvin Dunfee's General Store hanging on the wall in the Athens County Historical Society. I found Melvin's obituary in the files and discovered he was eighty-five years old when I had the chance to meet him, and he lived just four more years after that. He operated that store from 1923 until 1975, the year I met him. Whatever happened to the store and its contents is unknown, but I assume some other Dunfee folks claimed it because there were a slew of them populating East Athens County.

With jars procured, I drove by Cathy's house and spotted Miriam sitting on the front porch (sans banjo) just passing time. I approached the porch to tell her of my Ball Mason jar adventures and wondered if she was into canning. I was hoping for some help but I was not devoid of ulterior motives, with "ball" being the operative word. She silently pondered my request and then got up and said, "Let me throw a few things together and I'll come. Could you get me back tomorrow for classes by 11:00?"

"Sure," I said, but I thought, "perfect."

Miriam ducked into the house and soon emerged with a little cloth satchel that kinda looked like the handmade bag in which my grandmother kept her sewing supplies, at least the ones she did not keep between her breasts and inside her brassiere. I thought for a moment about the scissors, harmonica, elastic tape, ruler, knife, and other sundry essentials of life that grandmother Coonfield could retrieve at a moment's notice from her cleavage without a walk to another room. But quickly my attention turned back to my hippie woman companion and we headed to the wilds of Meigs County. Driving out of Albany, with the refrains of a Canned Heat song on the radio, I thought their name an apt description of my package nestled warmly in my pants, and as I lit up a doobie and passed it over to her, we sang along with them about water tasting like wine, and going up to the country, exactly where we were headed.

As we drove up, I asked Miriam if she wanted to cool off in the pond, but I knew the answer. She loved to swim, a fact that had come up in our party conversation. I grabbed a couple of towels, and we walked up the hill to the pond Mickey had built and stocked with fish. Why is taking ones clothes off outdoors just so satisfying? Why is watching a woman take off hers even more so? Miriam had on one of her prairie dresses and panties; I just my jeans and T-shirt. The water was warmed by summer heat, but still felt cool to our bodies. We splashed around, hugged a little, nibbled necks, and innocently frolicked in the water. We dressed in the long shadows of the cool of evening approaching, and walked hand-in-hand down the hill to the kitchen.

On the counter, picked that morning, were a few pounds of tomatoes, lots of zucchini, some green beans, peppers, and other garden delights. With John Denver on the stereo, roommates gone, a bottle of rosé uncorked, and the hot water bath heating on the stove, we peeled tomatoes, stringed the beans, sliced the zukes, and mostly sang to the tunes and boogied around the kitchen. Sweat soaked our hair, steam fogged the windows, twilight settled on the hills around the farmhouse, and I thought nothing was quite as sexy as a working, sweating woman in a hippie dress as the light of day fades in the sky and the excitement of night rises in one's soul, and other places. In the midst of canning, I roasted some chicken and made some crème bruleé (the old TCU Home Economics Gourmet Cooking Class for Men did come in handy). After a few hours of concentration, music, and some hot water burns, we were staring at about fifty jars of beautiful produce, including bread and butter zucchini, stewed tomatoes, hot pickled green beans, and an assortment of garden peppers. We lit up a doobie in honor and celebration of our achievements. Dope, the lubricant of the palate, the foreplay to gastronomic adventure, the appetizer of the mind, the cleanser of the colon, the alarm clock of the taste buds, the grass of greener gourmet pastures, the smoke of desire and ravenous hunger, the master of the munchies, and God's natural herb exclamation of bon appetite to the inhalant imbibers of the world. The chicken was done and the potatoes mashed. "Supper's on!" I declared.

Who is to know how long the meal took? Maybe it lasted for hours or maybe we devoured it in minutes, such is the nature of a head full of cannabis. Miriam and I retired to the living room with our crème bruleé as I put on the Bread let's-get-naked-and-get-it-on album with the song that always works.

Baby I'm-a want You
You the only one I care enough to hurt about
Maybe I'm-a crazy
But I just can't live without . . .

Your lovin' and affection
Givin' me direction [we used to karaoke this word as erection, of course]
Like a guiding light to help me through a darkest hour
Lately I'm a-prayin'
That you'll always be a-stayin' beside me
      (David Gates, "Baby I'm a Want You")

And a little later in the album, the coup de grace for wooing damsels to throw off their clothes and inhibitions.

No, you don't know me well,
In ev'ry little thing only time will tell,
If you believe the things that I do.
And we'll see it through.

Life can be short or long,
Love can be right or wrong,
And if I choose the one
I'd like to help me through,

I'd like to make it with you
I really think that we can make it girl.
      (David Gates, "Make it with You")

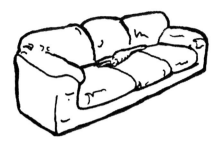

It was not long before the couch became an object of iniquity and lasciviousness. I suggested that we open up the hide-a-bed and get comfortable and my nature girl did not object. Miriam did not use deodorant and certainly did not douche, for her pits had the smell of yak and her pussy that of ripe cheese and tuna fish. Her body was soft and hairy; she was for me, without ever having yet known one carnally, a true Varmit lady and a free spirit of free love. Her eyes still spoke of vulnerability, responsiveness, appreciation, and "fuck me." The springs of the old couch left impressions on our bodies, the sheets became a tangled mess, and after either hours or minutes (hopefully not minutes for her and hours for me), our bodies fell asleep as Bread's last refrains faded out: "I really think that we could make it girl."

It was not often, certainly not nearly as often as I would have liked, that Miriam and I continued our country carnal escapades even though her friends warned me of her boyfriend whom I had once met, and rightfully feared. I always thought she deserved better. He was either just out of prison or just about to go in. A scary Appalachian type, his countenance recalled the dangers of *Deliverance* and the fear of amoral mountain people. He was older, he wasn't a student, and he emitted creepy vibes through his pores. Thankfully I survived our dalliances; I hope Miriam survived him.

Chapter 11: Love Art, Research, and Turkeys

It was my birthday, July 25th, and other than that, it was just a normal summer school day with a little party planned in the evening in my honor. The drive to Athens, always a mind-clearing cruise, took me yet again by the football stadium and basketball arena and up the hill to the academic part of the campus. A giant retaining wall, arching along the curved road, served as support to the buildings above. It also provided a massive flat surface for graffiti artists and paint-splashing hackers to express themselves below. The university long ago gave up the ridiculous notion that cleanliness is next to godliness, and unofficially relegated the wall to anyone and everyone who chose to express his inner Picasso. There were at times some disparaging words about specific people (mostly profs) that were quickly painted over, but "fuck" and "shithead" remained on the wall for weeks when not referencing anyone in particular. It was a haphazard mess of colors, slogans, and "I love you, Linda" statements. In gestalt, the huge wall resembled a Jackson Pollack canvas splashed with color and bold strokes. That is, of course, to give it the best of artistic interpretations. But not that day. On my birthday, the mix of graffiti was gone. In its stead was a white background some fifteen feet high and twenty feet long. In the center of the white background shone a giant sunburst in geometric design and 2-ft. letters saying, "Happy Birthday, Tango!" As I read the freshly painted sign, I swerved into the oncoming lane. Luckily, traffic was light or it might have been my last birthday. For you see "Tango" was me. It was the nickname bestowed upon me by Ben long before the Varmits tagged me with the label "Scoop" for my exploits on the softball diamond. Ben, the old Army guy, knew all the call letter names used in military communication and aviation. T-E-D stood for Tango Easy Dog, and he just shortened it to Tango. It fit, I liked it, and a handful of fellow grad students affectionately used it as my moniker.

Ben and Cathy were lurking around INCO halls when I arrived, looking like they had just pulled an all-nighter with bad drugs. They were checking me out, but I decided to play dumb, not an unusual occurrence.

"Did you notice anything coming into town today?" Cathy softly asked.

"Hmm, not really. Was I supposed to?" I said.

"Well, you know, on your drive up the hill to the campus, by the Chemistry building?"

"No, it looked the same to me," I lied.

They marched me down the hill and around the corner to *their* art work. Now of course, I had to reveal that I'd already seen it, but my surprise at the extent of their efforts was genuine. These two friends had started working on the birthday greeting as darkness fell with a gallon of paint, thinking they would knock it out in a couple of hours, but the project grew. Several gallons and many hours later, around 7:00 a.m., the masterpiece was done, only an hour before I drove by. My heart knew and recorded forever that love expresses itself in myriad ways, and I felt loved in spades. The greeting on that massive rough concrete retaining wall was another example of the power of Ben. Every day hence, as I drove past it or walked down to the gym for a few games of racquetball, I'd run my hand along the wall to feel the love, so to speak, and know never to take friendship for granted; it is a precious thing. At first, as new paint expressions appeared over my greeting, I felt a little sad. But as it began disappearing with "Go Bobcats" and other such renderings, I became more philosophical about the ebb and flow of life, the transient nature of our comings and goings, of opening ourselves up to new experiences while inadvertently, but nonetheless inherent in the act of turning toward something, turning our backs on those we leave behind, with memories most important indelibly burned in our brains, sometimes raw, sometimes lyrical, sometimes triggered by a smell, a sound, a song, a scene, but always ours to hold dear.

Summer school was finally over. Fall classes were only weeks away. Captain Crunch got a dorm job in town, Hip headed back to Kansas to work in the bike shop, and I found myself alone in the country without roommates. It should have been a worry, but I had a remodel on my mind. There was just enough time to fix up the bathroom, so I proceeded, despite not having Mickey and Anise's permission, for they were somewhere south of Mexico in their little Volvo sports car eating veggie enchiladas and kicking back a few margaritas. Better to ask forgiveness than permission, especially when the asking was impossible anyway.

As mentioned, the burlap-adorned walls were getting moldy. The burlap was rotting where it hung. The smell became overpowering, so off to the hardware store I went. Within days, the burlap was gone, a coffee-with-cream color paint job was in its place, new carpet lay on the floor, a designer shower curtain hung over the tub, and the rotten floor around the toilet had been replaced. More canning, some softball, and many an evening sitting out by the root cellar in an old dilapidated lawn chair with a Rolling Rock long neck in hand and lightning bugs twinkling in the deep dark beyond of the forest occupied my time and thoughts.

Another project needed my attention. Cranfield, now my steady canine companion, like all of God's creatures, had a tragic character flaw: he was scared shitless of storms, in general, and thunder, in particular. On three occasions that summer, when I was away at school and storms arose, I came home to find Cranfield hunkered down behind the couch shaking. As a mostly outside dog, his fearful path of entry to the security of the house was to rip the screen off of the outer door and claw the wooden kitchen door open, making shreds of it. I dutifully replaced the screen, sanded and painted the macerated door, and proudly felt accomplished. The next time, I felt a little angry. By the third time, I felt both incensed and stupid. This could not go on for long. I had long discussions with Cranfield, using brief psychotherapeutic techniques, Rogerian relational counseling, and even some Fritz Pearls gestalt therapy, to no avail.

"Cranfield, buddy, I know you are scared. Why, who wouldn't be? But you'll be safe on the porch outside here," I said with sympathy.

He'd listen attentively. I was lured into thinking the sessions were progressing nicely, when mid-sentence he'd circle three times, plop down on the grass, and begin licking his butt. I took that as a sign he was thinking about it. Or it could be a message that change for him was just not a priority. Doing the same thing over and over again and expecting different results was truly the mark of one crazy son-of-a-bitch, me, not him.

Cranfield's fears, bless his heart, were deep-seated and permanent. Something else had to change. So I took the front door off the hinges, sawed a rectangle in one of the lower panels, and hinged a swinging doggie door over the hole. Now, how to teach Cranfield to use the door? Treats are needed for good doggie training. The next day, after acquiring such, I was bound and determined to give poor Cranfield the option of coming and going without the fearful madness of destruction. I led Cranfield around to the front, showed him the treat, went inside the front room, got down on my knees, and called to him, while holding the treat next to the little door now cut into the larger one. Nothing. Cranfield laid down under the shade of the old oak tree. I kept calling to him, opened the pet door, held the treat out through it, and called him again. Nothing. He's asleep. I sat back on my haunches thinking of other alternatives. That's when the door opened nicely and in strolled Rutabaga, the yellow striped cat. This settled the argument about the intellectual prowess of cats versus dogs in my mind, but others will still argue it *ad infinitum*. "OK," I thought, "it is cool that the cats can come and go as they please, which is so very cat-like in nature anyway." I had only a few moments of contemplation when BANG, the door flew open and all 95 lbs of Cranfield came bolting through the door, knocking me over, and chasing Rutabaga into the kitchen. I yelled and screamed to no avail, but from that time on Cranfield, the cats, and a few other stray animals would come and go at will, rain or shine, sun or storm, cloudy or clear. The screen door and kitchen door stayed intact for the rest of my stay at The Country Place.

At the first meeting of the INCO graduate students, I met an older student returning to do his Ph.D. Dick had taught for many years in a little state college in Pennsylvania and now had boldly entered school in his fifties to round up his education and subsequent paycheck. After pleasantries, it was somehow determined that he did not have a place to park during graduate school and I offered him a look at The Country Place as an option. So, with a drive to Meigs County, a walk around the farm, a look at the corner bedroom and the newly remodeled bath, Dick said he liked the country, it would be quiet, the garden looked great, and it sure beat a dumpy dorm room in the Grad Quad of South Green. What a score: a roommate with money. He didn't smoke weed, wanted to study a lot, and didn't seem like the hustling-chicks type. I could afford to live at The Country Place for another year, and Dick seemed like a really nice guy.

The second year of graduate school takes on more mellow vibes than the stress-filled first. You start to know which classes you want to take from which professors, the fear factor has subsided, confidence is large, and many course requirements are behind you. A graduate teaching fellowship still paid my tuition and allowed me about $330 a month, enough for rent, food, beer, gas, and other incidentals. Luckily, I was healthy, and my folks took care of the cost for the infrequent doctor or dental visit. Varmit softball waned, but it was soon replaced by Varmit parties. They partied better than they played softball anyway. I became the grad assistant to a full professor, keeping his office hours, grading all his rhetoric papers, and generally being a slave to a stealthy university employee whom I saw twice during the semester. Oh yea, what a gig. He came to town to teach two classes and had me do all the dirty work. I kept his office hours, while he stayed home "writing and doing research." He hadn't published a book in fifteen years, but still drew a big salary, protected by tenure and tolerant deans.

This is too often the way of academia, a system finely honed in the dark ages. Even though big campuses command big revenues from state legislators, they remain in the proverbial managerial and leadership dark ages. Much lip service is given to the virtue of the university community, but too often isolation, mistrust, ego, lack of collaboration, selfishness, and me-first thinking typifies the zeitgeist of the institution. And Ohio University in the mid 1970s was no exception. That is not to say that wonderful, dedicated people did not reside within its hallowed walls. There were many professors who made student learning their *a priori* priority, worked extra hard counseling students, did significant research, and served on university committees. What I found most curious was how the university selected new presidents, deans, and even faculty. They would take months to form a search committee, advertise the position, pore over countless resumes, select a number to interview, discuss the finalists *ad nauseum*, develop favorites, bring them to campus to meet everyone including the janitor, argue on their behalf, and after a year, sometimes two, some Mr. Dean (it was always a guy back then) would make an arbitrary and capricious decision selecting his favorite candidate, sometimes not even one in the top three selected by the committee, and the announcement would come out in the school paper to everyone's surprise. Welcome to the dark ages of managerial enlightenment.

Ben, Rick, and I, amidst long scholarly discussions, decided together during one of those dialectics that the field of listening in communication studies was woefully inadequate. Most previous studies had focused on listening as memory, like hearing a string of numbers and remembering them, but this is much more a cognitive function than it is true listening.

We thought listening was therapeutic, powerful, caring, essential to authentic communication, and mandatory in the difficult development of relationship building. So Rick, Ben, and I started meeting early on Saturday mornings. It was much more of a commitment for me to travel the needed thirty minutes from the farm after a Friday night of partying than it was for them to just roll out of beds warmed by wives and walk either a block or fifty feet to meet. In any case, we got together. We developed a construct, as they say in the research field, and called it "empathic listening."

It had to do with how one hears the language of feelings, understands it empathically, and responds to it appropriately. Counselors, psychiatrists, doctors, teachers, spouses, friends, therapists, and others make a living, heal, or grow to love others via empathic listening. We were onto something powerful. With one published article in the bag and an accepted paper at a national communication conference for the fall of 1974, our construct took shape in the form of the Human Empathic Listening Test, geared for crisis intervention counselors dealing with raw human emotions on the phone daily. Subsequently, we sold hundreds of tests to suicide intervention call centers, drug help lines, and similar organizations, while publishing several more articles and taking "special studies" courses where our research got rewarded with college credit and faculty support.

Ben was the counselor and planner, Rick served as the statistics guru, and I filled in around the edges doing research, writing papers, and "go-fering," doing the needed tasks such as obtaining business cards, stationery, preparing mailings, and fulfilling orders. It was rich plantings in the garden of academia, the fruit of our extracurricular activities its own reward. It taught me that I work better in groups, with deadlines, commitments, and a community of shared expectations. Given the solitary task of writing and researching alone, I tend to find a thousand other things to do, with procrastination my friend and ultimate enemy, when responsibility all resides within self. It's a bitch being human.

One of our colleagues, Fred, a lovable, but quasi-obnoxious little guy from Indiana, chided me to round out my fowl menagerie by adding a slew (or whatever the term is) of turkeys to my gaggle of geese and flock of chickens. Maybe it's a good thing this country did not go with the terminally stupid turkey as our national symbol, for it would have been way too symbolic given the acts and decisions we have made as a nation over the years. It is no wonder Fred loved turkeys, as the younger and more conservative among us, he would rise every morning and state emphatically in the mirror, "Day by day in every way, I become greater and greater. I AM FRED!!!" Gobble, gobble! He was just doing a Ph.D. so he could go back to Indiana and run for governor and drive the liberals crazy. He became infamous for his Fred's Famous Bean Delight, a green bean casserole made in the Midwest style with canned green beans, Campbell's Cream of Mushroom soup poured over the top, and a can of fried onion crisps sprinkled on top. Like the surety of the sunrise, any grad student potluck would have Fred's Bean Delight sitting there for consumption, with him standing proudly by to dish it up.

So it was no surprise when he presented me with a little box of ten turkey poults, about the same size as the little yellow chicks sold in Five & Dime stores back in Oklahoma around Easter time.

"Now what the fuck do I do with ten little whatever they're called?" I scolded.

"Turkeys, you turkey. You raise 'em and we eat 'em," he matter-of-factly stated. "I'll help you with feed, all you need in a little pen to keep them in."

What could I say? They were innocent little critters. I did have a little shed/pen combo next to the goose house, and what the hell, not knowing anything about how to do something hadn't stopped me before. So with five lbs. of feed in hand and a box of chirping baby turkeys in tow, I headed to the country to figure out housing and feeding arrangements for the centerpiece of Thanksgiving dinner. That evening I patched up the holes in the little rundown shed, to keep the turkeys in and the vermin out. I found an old, long, tin poultry trough for watering and I raked the grass in the pen so these little suckers would not get lost in the high grass. Now, of course, I could not put them directly out in the elements at such a young and tender age. Oh no, they had to reside in the corner of the house near the oil-burning stove and squawk all night long until they either got bigger or until I shot or strangled them one by one with malice and delight.

Did I say how stupid turkeys are? They are not smart enough to know how to drink water, so I had to put marbles in the little bowl, and when they pecked at the marbles out of curiosity they would inadvertently drink water in order to stay alive. As they reached softball size, I put them out in the pen during the day to acclimate them to the great outdoors. At night they still stunk up the kitchen and screeched loudly, but it seemed like the right thing to do.

As it turned out, after a couple of successful weeks in the outdoor abode, a storm brewed over the plains of Ohio and dumped buckets on Copperhead Hollow. This fascinated the turkeys who looked to the excitement in the skies and opened their mouths in amazement, thereby drowning to death. "Brothers and sisters, your dearly departed have reduced your ranks to seven, and it's survival of the fittest time for all of you." I told them directly. A couple of mornings later I went out to feed them and found feathers everywhere, mixed with blood and guts. Chicken coop attack déjà vu all over again. Even though I thought my young feathered friends were safely locked in the turkey shed for the night, a creature had dug underneath the board siding and mastered a hole big enough to crawl through and wreck havoc on the victims of his feast. I said to them, "Brother and sisters, our ranks are now down to five, and we know it's a dog-eat-dog world and we have bone meal shorts. Brace yourself for other possible impending doom." Two others died in the next few weeks of unknown causes, for I had fixed the shed to my satisfaction with a whole strand of chicken wire buried with rocks around the perimeter. Eventually three of the chicks made it to adulthood. Batting 300 will get you into the Baseball Hall of Fame, but it seemed much too drastic a toll on the oh-so-stupid, but innocent nonetheless, feathered friends.

The INCO chairperson called me into his office and after buttering me up with lots of nicey-nicey talk (about my positive student evaluations). He said I would be perfect to represent the College of Communication on the Graduate Student Council of the university. The position offered grad assistant money without a teaching load and only required one meeting a month.

"How hard could that be?" I thought to myself.

"I'm your man, Dr. B. What's the next step?"

He gave me a piece of paper with the meeting info on it and in a few days, at the appointed time, I headed across the main green to the administration building. The graduate dean sat in on the meetings and served as an advisor. Attending were the officers and a dozen or so members from various colleges of the university. Whoa, did I forget that grad students are quite navel-staring, busy, selfish, mostly loners, and not really into governance, whatever there was to govern anyway. Needless to say, the discussions were inane and the topics meaningless, even though the Council had concocted rationalizations for their purpose and importance. This knowledge of how groups do this would serve me well as a consultant in later years. An agenda item at this meeting was the election of a vice-president, for another candidate, brighter than the others, had bailed. No one volunteered, and in a moment of either weakness or brilliance, I raised my hand and became the royal number two Gumby of a do-nothing group of ne'er-do-wells. Little did I know that that act alone would help mold my life, for better or worse.

Chapter 12: Fall Leaves and the Fall Crop

Shocking the world, but not as much as me, I excelled in the twelve hours of Ph.D. statistics required for my degree. I took lots of courses from other departments, from sociology, guidance and counseling, psychology, and, of course, INCO. The fall leaves of Southeast Ohio, certainly not known worldwide like New England, still held their magic. Enough deciduous trees, given cool temperatures and the right amount of rain, speckled the hillsides with the autumn colors that so make glad the heart of man. Problem is, they also stack up around the house and must be raked out of the way. So in my best Tom Sawyer style, I convinced Dr. Dave and his girlfriend, Amy, to come out for dinner and a leaf raking party.

I met Dr. Dave when we both lived in the South Green Dorms at the central "cafeteria" that served a number of buildings. He did not fit the stereotype of an undergraduate. He always wore a recycled postal worker jacket, sported an extra long and full beard, and pretty much kept to himself. Come to find out, he was exactly my age; he had been to college in St. Louis for a while before dropping out, buying a Harley, and going on the road to find himself and discover America, à la *Easy Rider*. He labored in some steel mills and worked as a mail carrier (hence the jacket's authenticity). Then, just like Forrest Gump, he stopped running, in his case traveling, and decided to become a medical doctor. It was a long shot at best for this tattered soul from a large and dysfunctional family, but he had a heart of gold and always recounted interesting travel stories. So it was that I invited him and his hippie girlfriend, Amy, to a country respite. Now I needed a date to round out the party. The initial fall meetings that the newbie grad students had to attend presented the opportunity for this veteran to troll the new coeds for the "date-ables." I honed in on Debbie, a master's student fresh out of undergrad who fancied my rap about living in the country, growing a garden, and hanging out on a farm. It did not take long for the plan to work. The four of us took off early Saturday afternoon and commenced to rake up a humongous pile of leaves behind the house. Like little kids throughout the world, at least where they have leaves, we began to jump, throw leaves at each other, romp and wrestle around, and laugh and frolic with abandon. Jonathan Edwards's national anthem of Athens County was blaring out the open windows and we sung along. Each one of us sang a verse while the others sucked up a big toke from the doobie.

Way down in Athens County
that's where I am
Going on the road tomorrow
Up to Amsterdam
Way down in Athens County
Stop and have some wine
Athens County
Marie and Me, We're doin' fine
Sweet Maria
Never Long Gone
Sweet Maria
Never long gone, never long gone.
    (Jonathan Edwards and Joseph Dolce, "Athens County")

Luckily, we kept the lit doobies and the leaves separate. With tunes ablaze, minds abuzz, the fall light fading, and a harvest moon arising, we cooked up some dinner. After supper as we sat around the living room drinking beer and smoking dope, I wondered if I was going to have to make a trip to Athens late at night to return Debbie to her abode or if the stars could align for a night of love. Well, they sort of aligned. Debbie and I headed up the narrow staircase to see where cosmic karma might take us. Debbie had a rounded face, giant tits, and a narrow waist, provocative but slightly out of proportion. She was very attractive, slightly mysterious, and secretive. I thought that honesty and a little caution might get me some action with what was before me on the bed. But despite the excitement of leaf jumping, dope-smoking, tune-listening, song-singing, good food-eating, and being the free loving hippies of the era, "first date" syndrome still abided in the heart of this young woman who harbored some notions of propriety and rightness. We got naked and made out a little, but I quickly surmised that sex on the first date was clearly out of the question. But there is nothing wrong with mutual nudity with a warm, smart, and big-breasted woman. It certainly beat sleeping alone. The cool of the fall morning air filled the loft while the electric blanket kept Debbie and me cozy. Watching her dress and go from white skin and bushy bush to tight jeans and tighter top stretched around those enormous globes, made me think of life someday in a relationship, and what that would be like. If this was any precursor, well, it wouldn't be a bad life at all.

The next weekend, I headed down to Bob's house to score some milk topped with a few cups of heavy cream from Betsy, their faithful cow. The only leaves holding onto the limbs were brown and sparse. Damp air settled in the hollows as I drove around the bend and headed up the driveway to the ramshackle shack they called home. Affectionately named The Hilltop, it was, duh, on a hill. Of course, half of Meigs County was on a hill and the other half in the valley, but I guess it was important to differentiate.

"Scoop! Scoop!" echoed out of the holes in the walls as Bob recognized the car and hailed a hearty hello. He had a couple of gallons of milk for sale, and for ceremony and camaraderie he passed me a cigar-sized mind bomb of Meigs County finest. When I was about half done, Bob said that he wanted to show me something and I followed him to the barn. He opened two locks and pulled back the door. The aroma hit me head on. There hung from the rafters, the hay loft, the walls, and the 2 x 4s nailed to the cross beams, thousands of marijuana plants: the fall crop. Some of the plants were ten feet in length, a foot wide, and sticky to the touch. It was overwhelming; the smell assaulted the nostrils, alternating between the sweet smell of grass and the pungent smell of THC. Bob smiled proudly, leaning against the barn door. All I could say was, "HOLY SHIT!" Bob chuckled. I was now privy to information closely-guarded, but shared with a trusted colleague. Although I operated in a different world in academic Athens, I felt the weight of the sacred trust.

"It'll be a couple more weeks before they are ready to go." Bob stated.

"What will you do with all this dope?" I inquired.

Bob looked at me with that sideways glance of his, and, with the perfected method of answering a question honestly without really telling you anything, responded, "We have our Varmit distribution system that'll take care of it." I took him at his word and did not need to know more.

Decades later, I would hear stories about the time when warnings of a raid filtered to The Hilltop and in frantic Keystone Kop-like manner, the pot was gathered up, thrown haphazardly into an old truck, and hauled to a barn near Varmit State Park. As they fled bouncing down the hilly highways of Meigs County, thousands of dollars of pot flew out and became detritus to rot with the leaves in the drainage ditches. A few days later, they learned that all the pot had been ripped off and they were left with nothing but an empty barn and a cashless winter.

I asked about the caged chickens behind the barn. Bob smiled another wily one and motioned me to follow him. Pinned in behind multiple 4 x 4-foot fences with a little shelter to have relief from the weather, stood a bunch of beautiful roosters each inhabiting its own fenced condo.

"Fighting cocks," Bob said.

My head was already spinning with THC, which made reality a little shaky and verbal skills suspect, and now I was moving at the speed of psychotropic drugs to a royal mind fuck. First, a giant barn doubling as a weed-drying rack, and now, a flock of fighting cocks, trained as killers, nasty by nature, and being raised by someone I considered a friend. Some combination of friendship, academic "participant observation," open-mindedness or naïveté, conspired to help me accept that this was the life of a Varmit of Meigs County. Who was I to question what went on in these hills?

"Where do the cocks fight?" I asked.

"Oh we have a ring in a barn not far from here where we put 'em to the test," Bob honestly answered without too much detail.

"Are you worried about getting caught?" I inquired.

"Sheriff Bob down in Pomeroy hates criminals, but doesn't much care about stuff that's good for the economy of Meigs County. We're outlaws, not criminals."

It was subtle, but I was beginning to understand the difference.

We walked back to the car with me holding a gallon of milk in each hand and Bob putting his arm around my shoulder, I think to reassure me. In a stream of consciousness sort of way he talked of this being a good year; this is just our life, not to justify but to highlight, not with guilt or embarrassment but rather matter of factly, just the life of a Varmit. Back at the ranch, as I shook the cream into butter, it came to me that not many people have ever been to a cock fight. As abhorrent as it might seem, the notion intrigued me, for what is youth without adventure?

Chapter 13: If Winter Comes, Can Spring Be Far Behind

Winter rain, now tell me why
Summers fade and roses die
The answer came, the wind and rain

Golden hills, now veiled in gray
Summer leaves have blown away
Now what remains, the wind and rain.

Same old friend the wind and rain
(We'll see summer by and by)
Winter gray and falling rain
(Summers fade and roses die)
We'll see summer come again
(Like a song that's born to soar the sky)
  (Eric Anderson and Bob Weir, "Weather Report Suite: Part 1")

In winter, life turns inward. The trees and plants keep food reserves in their roots and sap as low as possible to brace against the chill, like humans clutch coats and scarves up close around collars to protect precious inner warmth, like the forest creatures hibernate in closed confines and limit their activity; all of us waiting for spring to unfold and give us new life. The outdoors are just a necessity to bear as people go from one warm place to another, the winter garden is just a few wet and moldy stalks with little resemblance to the lush green of the growth months, and farm life consists of only the most essential tasks: feeding animals, making sure the well pump works, and, well, that's about it. Every once in a while I would chop some kindling from the cords of wood stacked up by the house but even then it was quick and business-like. I did not want to trifle with the cold Norse gods.

Joe was a fellow grad student who had entered school the previous winter term after having finished a master's degree and teaching some in college. The two of us decided to do indoor stuff ourselves. We ordered some spores from a mail order house and a week or so later they arrived, to our delight, a little package of grains so small as to be invisible to our eyes. But we knew they were there. It was not illegal to order spores of *psilocybe cubensis,* commonly known as "psilocybin," or even more commonly known as "magic mushrooms" or "golden top." This psychoactive, psychedelic, hallucinogenic mushroom is known in Mexico as San Isidro Labrador, after the patron saint of plowing; in Mazarec as "di-xi-tjo-le-rra-ja," the "divine mushroom of manure"; in Thailand as "hed keequai," the mushroom that appears after the water buffalo shits; and in Holland as "the gigglehead," for really obvious reasons understood by imbibers. The sixties saw cults of "shroom" eaters, shamanic believers of its powers to connect one with cosmic forces of the universe. *High Times* magazine featured many an article on how to order spores, grow the little critters, and enjoy them safely. Joe held such an article in his hand. I had procured the growing medium: rye wheat, gypsum, and several other ingredients commonly found in the kitchens of America. Like cheese-making, one had to avoid germs, yeast, and other little things that grow in and contaminate cultured mediums, so sterilization was essential to insure that the spores had free reign to grow at will without competing with other wanton interlopers.

The production reminded me of canning, for we prepared the food stuff to go in sterile jars, sealed them up tight, and water-bathed them to a right hot boil for twenty minutes in order to massacre stray and unwanted nastiness. With the last of the jars inoculated with the spores and sealed quickly to avoid contamination, Joe and I sat in his kitchen and admired our winter garden. Opening a cheap bottle of Italian wine (Joe's heritage), I retrieved out of the oven a New Orleans dish of baked crab and cheese, a real treat for grad students who swear a vow of poverty when entering school. Viewing our labors while we ate, I thought of Herman Hesse who had Siddhartha speak so profoundly in his book of the same name: "I can work and I can wait. I have worked, now is the time to wait."

Despite our best efforts, we lost a few jars to green, gloppy growth, probably the cure for cancer, but garbage to our intent. With patience and time, we successfully nurtured over three quarters of the jars to fruition. The mushrooms were brown, spindly little things with pointy little penis-like heads on top, sending out spidery filament legs to soak up the nutrients below.

Joe air-dried some and cured some in a hydrator, ending up with nearly weightless curly masses of dried mushrooms. The aroma both intrigued the palate and alienated the gut. Many folks report when ingesting this particular species of mushrooms experiencing a gag reflex, a reaction I confirmed. Psilocybin is 100 times *less* potent than LSD and ten times *more* potent than mescaline, the active ingredient in peyote cactus. I learned that psilocybin belongs to a class of chemicals called indole alkaloids, or tryptamines, all similar to serotonin. I like the "tryp" word; it is in function appropriately designated. Luckily, the extreme majority of mushrooms that contain psilocybin are quite consistent in content of the active hallucinogen, about 1%, creating the same pharmacological effects throughout the world. There are over 186 known species of magic mushrooms around the globe, with 76 of them reportedly growing in Mexico alone. Murders, drug wars, highly-guarded secret harvesting spots, and lots of cow shit on boots parallels the rise of mushrooms as a high of choice among the adventure-seekers of the tie-dyed world. I was just curious. Timothy Leary aside, I was living the adage of Jerry Jeff Walker's lyrics:

> "Gettin' by on gettin' bys *(we sang high's)* my stock and trade
> Living it day by day
> Picking up the pieces wherever they fall
> Just letting it roll, letting the high times carry the low
> I'm just living my life easy come, easy go."

With a whole wall full of canning jars filled with the bounty of the garden, now rounded out by several jars of brown little buggers growing on what resembled pure snow, I was ready for winter. Ben, Rick, and I continued our research, writing, and selling our listening test to crisis-intervention centers around the country and even a few foreign countries. I was taking courses in numerous departments, the surviving turkeys had reached full growth, and the geese were still obnoxious. Dick and I kept mostly separate lives of friendly respect as roommates. Hunkering down in the books consumed my time and energy. In conversations with Dr. W., we got interested in a student chapter of the American Society of Training and Development (ASTD), the national organization of training and development professionals. There were a handful of student chapters, and we thought why not here? So we wrote Articles of Incorporation, created a charter, solicited members, and I became the organization's first president. That honor came with a trip to Madison, Wisconsin, ASTD's corporate headquarters, for a leadership class focusing on how to run and grow a chapter. I came home to conduct monthly meetings to try learning about how the real world of work worked, how to transition from academia to the corporate world, and what skills one needed to do training and development out there in the real world of employment. Ben and Weezie still put up with me at their home, in spite of my other life of wayward beer drinking, dope-smoking, 'shroom-growing, coed-screwing, softball-playing Varmit types. In contrast, I also loved my time at their holy house of home-cooking, football-watching, pillow-lounging, casserole-eating, serious-discussion-and-uncontrollable-laughter-shrine of Midwestern civility. Every Wednesday evening, I became a patron of the arts and an avid supporter of the Athens International Film Festival, previewing the latest porn escapades on the screen of lascivious, libertine, libidinous, loose, lustful, and even lecherous artwork. Ah, X marked the spot.

Once a month I'd trudge over to the administration building for the Grad Council meetings, wondering what the hell had I gotten myself into, and trying to make sense of how this not-so-august group could gain a mission, become relevant to someone, and maybe, oh just maybe, do something of import in the realm of academia.

Many a night after library work, the INCO grad group would gather at the Tavern to drink a few beers and bemoan the weirdness of professors and the burden of our workload. Every once in a while, Cathy and I would dance to Roberta Flack's lonesome song, "Killing Me Softly." Cathy could dance quite wonderfully, unless she had reached the tipping point of just too much beer, and then catching her before she stumbled became more important than swaying to the lyrics of a sensuous song. One evening after library work, pitchers at the Tavern, a few spins around the dance floor, and a very cold walk around the block to smoke some new reefer that had been circulating around campus, I headed home toward the country, destined to the cold confines of the upper room alone, the attic that served as my bedroom. The system, as I called it, was honed to a fine process. First thing, go upstairs and turn on the electric blanket. Now some might think me a wuss for using an electric device to stay cozy in the dead of winter. But fuck 'em, it was way too cold up there for any stack of blankets and self-warming to do the trick. I even learned to sleep under the covers, because pulling nose hairs out by the icicles made one search for creative ways to avoid morning pain. Then I would come back down and stand by either the oil stove in the kitchen or the wood stove in the dining room, whichever was warmer. I'd light the gas stove and boil up some water for tea, and just as the last bit of hot liquid coated the throat I knew the bed would be warm and sleep imminent. Sometimes I would utter the words of Shakespeare as I braced myself for the cold reality of the walk up the stairs: "The innocent sleep, sleep that knits up the ravel'd sleave of care, the death of each day's life, sore labor's bath, balm of hurt minds, great nature's second course, chief nourisher in life's feast."

But I was not home yet, just leaving Athens heading out Highway 50 toward Albany. Driving after drinking was not smart, but somehow I had managed to be successful at it even though alcohol makes stupid monsters of us all. Driving after drinking and smoking is probably doubly dumb, but I discovered that dope actually mellowed me out and slowed me down. Although, ultimately it just left a slower, stupider driver to negotiate the curves of Meigs County. Driving along with the radio on and my mind spacing out between music and thoughts, just cruising a few miles south of Albany in the heart of the rolling farmland so prevalent in Ohio and *bam*, I hit something.

Reality mostly blurs during surprise and shock, but reality slows one's thoughts in time of crisis and I found time to glance off to my right to spot a farm pond and a few geese. Instinctively as well, I glanced in the rearview mirror and saw a white object on the road. Did I hit a goose? Was it something else? Am I watching death in the rearview mirror, or what? Was that a cry I heard at impact, and squawking in the ever increasing distance? They do not call them mind-altering drugs for nothing. I could not be sure what was actually transpiring, and the fear and flight response drove me onward, unsure of what was behind me. Rationalizations took over: "Oh, it was probably a bag of trash; I couldn't do anything even if I stopped; What if the farmer had a gun? It's just maybe a silly goose for God's sake." My mind ran through them quickly. But my heart was racing, sweat wet my brow, and my hands began shaking on the wheel. I drove on. Hell bent for leather I drove on just wanting to be somewhere else, just wanting whatever it was behind me, just wanting to be experiencing a different reality, whatever it might be.

I made it to Carpenter, rounded the turn, and as I started to accelerate after the turn I spotted the old tree, big and brooding and staring right at me. I slowed even further and just stopped. The branches, bare of leaves but still big on expanse, shadowed my car in the moonlight. My head dropped down into my cupped hands on the steering wheel and I began to cry, which soon led to abject sobbing, followed by gasping for air. I let out a bloodcurdling scream of cowardly anguish, fear, self-hatred, sadness, and anger, all rolled into one. The tree offered no solace, but did not stand in judgment either. I had seen death in the butchered farm animals killed for food before, and death is death, but I caused this one, needlessly I thought. Would it make any difference if it was an accident, certainly not purposeful? Is it any wonder that my classmates who fought in Vietnam had come back fucked up? Jeez, I just killed a goose and they burned down villages of innocent people. Drugs, suicide, inability to hold down a job, divorce, alcoholism, dropping out, all results of war-time experiences, and I felt this way for killing a goose. Would it have been different if I had not been drinking or smoking dope? Who knows? But I have no other choice than the reality that haunts me today. The therapeutic 16-mile drive from The Country Place to Athens and back gained a mid-trip reality vignette. I never passed that pond without a feeling of guilt, regret, pain, and disappointment in self creeping or just slamming into my consciousness. Life goes on after death, although it alters us forever.

Chapter 14: One Big Turkey, One Big Test

It was a new year, 1975, winter term had started, and I got word of a big Varmit party down in South County. Bob said that they were cooking a fatted calf and that I should bring something of the potluck variety. I suggested a turkey; he said "bring it on." So out to the turkey pen with ax in hand I went at dusk the day before the party. There were three left, and given the grain they had devoured over the months, they were humongous. Twenty pounds of bird at Thanksgiving feeds a lot of friends and family, but these birds had left that size behind a long time before. I grabbed one by the neck and it flapped around frenetically with feathers flying in a flurry. As dead weight it was probably like a 40-lb sack of flour, but with feathers, feet and wings, and struggling for life, it was like I was wrestling a pissed off 120-lb bale of live, wild ass hay. Somehow I got the neck centered on the stump and with a giant swing severed the head. Thump!! But it was not over yet. Everyone has heard the old farm adage, "running around like a chicken with its head cut off." Well, like a chicken on steroids that critter flopped around with blood spurting out in buckets as it clung to life and raced to death. The scene went on for what seemed like an interminable time. Picture me matching the craziness of the turkey. I was running around like a chicken with its head cut off trying to avoid a blood bath, literally.

Finally, hours later, OK, maybe seconds later, the turkey's spirit finally went to the great beyond. I sighed with big relief. The other two birds stood as statues of shock, and I felt less for the dead than the living. "Let's get this bird outta here quick," I thought.

Plucking a huge bird is no easy task. The hot water needed to dip it into requires a very large container and there were none to be found on the farm. I threw the guts to Cranfield, salvaged the liver, and scraped the remaining feathers off with a knife, using as much hot water as I could boil on the stove and pour on the feathers to loosen them up. When I had finished, it looked like someone had tried to shave drunk and did a really lousy job. I thought about getting little pieces of toilet paper and placing them on each puncture wound, as any self-respecting man who shaves with a razor knows how to do. But I kyboshed that idea pretty quickly, and I placed some bags of ice on the dead bird to ebb the flow of red. Luckily it was cold enough in the root cellar to cure the bird till the next day, for the fridge, woefully too small, would not accommodate this very large lump.

Finding farms in the dark in Meigs County is not for the faint of heart, or directionally-challenged. Perfect directions, even written down still produce utterances such as, "Where the fuck is this place?" But I knew I was close when the aroma of roasting beef in the form of half a side of cow caught my olfactory attention.

"What the fuck is that?" Bob exclaimed upon laying eyes on the giant creature I was struggling to carry into the kitchen.

"A turkey," I deadpanned.

"How many turkeys, did you say?" Bob responded.

"Here, help me carry this in."

That's when I glanced down at the stove, an old-fashioned porcelain one with a tiny little oven off to one side. I am not sure that grandma's cornbread would have fit in there, much less a bird that took two young men to carry into the kitchen.

"When will the beef steaks be done?" I inquired.

"Not till this evening, we're just partying until then," Bob replied.

"You got a big knife around here somewhere," I asked.

Bob produced a knife, not sharp enough to cut cream and not big enough to take on a giant pterodactyl.

"How 'bout a saw from the barn, anything there we could use," I asked again.

"What the hell you goin' do with a saw?" he quizzed.

"I'm goin' cut the bird in half so it'll fit in the oven," I stated.

So with saw in one hand and the bloodily skinned turkey held in the other, like a surgeon in war time on the frontline of life and death, I sawed that bird in half, splitting the breast bone. Bob held on for dear life trying not to lose a finger (or arm) in the process. With a final slice of the saw on some loose skin, one half of the bird plopped on the floor and the other half-nestled safely in our hands. We crammed it into the oven with not a little bit of persuasion. I turned the antique dial to 350 degrees.

"OK, this puppy will be ready to eat about the same time as the cow," I exclaimed. The other half of the turkey was cut up like a cadaver in the morgue and doled out on a first come, first served basis to eager Varmits who would enjoy turkey sandwiches for weeks.

Varmit parties are not easy to describe; simple words don't quite capture the phenomenon. Beer, cheap wine, and a variety of Meigs's finest are passed around. Conversational topics include softball, what's happening with local farmers, drug-running, athletic prowess, the cash crop (past and upcoming), card games, and cow diseases (not easy listening with a roasting one a few feet away). There was ribbing, kidding, poking jabs, joke telling, and various attempts at humor, much of it scatological and sexual. The ladies mostly kept to themselves, with intermittent rendezvous of male/female recognition, even affection. Topics seemed to repeat often, stories got better throughout the day, and roaches piled up in the ashtray on the picnic table while beer bottles accumulated in the corner of the yard.

At supper time, giant bowls of salads, potatoes, green beans, stewed tomatoes, and other delights from the summer's garden and the local grocery store magically appeared. Without fanfare, prayer, ceremony, or even manners, the Varmits dug in and it was every man (and I do mean man) for himself. Eating is a pretty basic human need, primal in intent, necessary for survival. Had the Varmits eaten in weeks? You would have never known it given the amount of food that quickly disappeared like lines on an Etch-A-Sketch. Hunks of beef were cut off in odd shapes and with no butchery logic, and the roasted bird was literally torn apart by greasy hands before my very eyes. Women and children came last. The cavemen-like behaviors were both charming and gross. But never have I seen before or since such unbridled exuberance expressed in stuffing one's face as I observed in the Varmits that evening. I chuckled and rolled my eyes at French Fry; she smiled that knowing smile and shrugged her shoulders, and we, for that moment, saw the world the same, as ironic and humorous as it was.

A year or so later, when I had moved back to the South Green to live, my then girlfriend, Palmer, brought back some lobsters from her home in Maine. I invited a few Varmits over to my little apartment to enjoy the famous New England crustacean. The primordial instincts once again consumed the Varmits as they ripped into the boiled tails, butter dripping from their chins.

"If it's free, it's for me," Bob said. The Varmits strike again. But with plenty of appreciation and praise, they departed and headed down to Harpo's bar for a few brews. Palmer and I were left with the leg meat to pick and enjoy, a task much too tedious for a Varmit bent on good food fast.

"If winter comes can spring be far behind?" Shelley the poet wrote. It was the end of the second year of my program, and the required classes were almost completed. I had to put together a committee for my doctoral comprehensive exam, a group of professors required by academic tradition to make you feel as stupid as possible. I acquired a couple of INCO profs, a Guidance and Counseling one, and a reluctant, Rogerian non-rat psychologist from the Psychology Department. My major professor and I collaborated on how many hours and on what subjects I would write for each gentleman, and a comp plan was written up and distributed to each of them. They in turn, had weeks to deviously plan my demise, conjuring up unanswerable questions about which, I, in turn, would, over the course of a week, write something erudite. So the subjects I needed to prepare for were limited to a handful of topics such as rhetoric, interpersonal communication, organizational communication, Synectics, counseling techniques, sociology of organizations, and communication as dialogue. Ben, Rick, and I continued our research, I put classes on cruise control, and I, one scared rat, decided that early May brilliance would have to be created in February, March, and April.

With an illegal number of books checked out of the library (I think I used another student's card), another stack borrowed from professors, and some from my own collection, I began the life of a country hermit: turning down parties, abstaining from screw fests with Miriam, foregoing imbibing at the Tavern, neglecting support of the International Athens Film Festival, and missing my normal hours on the couch of Ben and Weezie's therapeutic emporium. Instead, I hunkered down for the longest all-nighter of my life, three months of cramming, reading, note-taking, scanning, and memorizing. Nothing before, nor since, had, or could, nor did, compare with that focused intellectual intensity. Dick allowed me to take over the dining room table next to the chrome pot-bellied stove that kept me warm and cozy, just the opposite of the frigid upstairs attic bedroom.

Picture three stacks of books on the floor rising up past the table top, and I needed to know a lot about each one of them to successfully pass my comps. Contemplating that daunting task one stormy evening, my mind overloaded and frazzled, it was all I could do to trudge up the steep stairs and fall into bed. I counted the number of seconds for each thunder clap to arrive after the lightning illuminated the attic, laying there knowing that the storm was fast approaching Copperhead Hollow. Those who have not experienced a Midwestern lightning and thunder storm, like most Oregonians, haven't fully come to meet the face-to-face the power of Mother Nature, and she can be a bitch. Yep, it's truly electrifying, literally, slightly scary, totally involving, with elements of the unknown, unanticipated, and unwanted. And that is exactly what happened in less than a split second. The brightest light of my life flashed like a meteorite had landed a few feet away from the bed, but that might have been less a blow than what actually happened. An old oak tree grew about ten feet outside of my attic window, its leaves and limbs shading the whole side of the house and lapping over the roof. At that very moment, lightning lasered the largest branching limb of that tree. Nature's force severed, splintered, and mutilated that foot-and-a-half wide piece of timber. The sound, although lasting only milliseconds, hit me like a cross between a lobotomy and electric shock treatments. I felt as if I was standing at ground zero of an atomic bomb drop with forty machine guns going off within inches of my ears, with a simultaneous dynamite explosion erupting. Actually, it was louder than that. Just then, I saw out the window a wire burning and sizzling rapidly and zipping toward the house like someone had lit the fuse of a pile of dynamite. It ended in a mini explosion at the phone outlet in the bedroom just inches from my bed and started a small fire. I experienced absolute terror and befuddlement as I lay there in the stinky smoke. My heart stopped. Then silence. Dead silence. Luckily the flame extinguished itself quickly, so I jumped out of bed and raced downstairs to see if Dick was OK. As he rushed out of his room I asked if he was OK. I saw him mouth the words, "I'm fine, how about you?" I knew he said those words for I read his lips, but no sound registered in my brain. I asked him to say something else with repeated results. I banged my hand on my head, and other than the reverberations through my hand, arm, and body, I heard nothing.

"My God, am I deaf?" I thought in silence. Then I discovered that I could hear in one ear slightly. Turning my good ear to Dick, I asked him if he could hear.

"Not very well," he responded. "I think it'll be temporary," he continued, noticing the shock on my face and speculating that I'd experienced the same. We talked for a little while longer while the rain beat down on the slate roof and hammered the windows. It is not easy going back to bed after one has taken such a hit to the body: nerves electrified, blood vessels fried, brain shocked, muscles twitching, and sinew aflame. With the residual smell of smoke in the air, I noticed Cranfield huddled in the corner shaking fearfully and looking at me and saying with his eyes, "What the hell was that?" I crept over to him, sat down on the floor, softly petted his head and ears, and told him he'd be alright, too.

For several days, I needed to turn my head sideways to hear with my good ear, but after a while the ringing subsided and my hearing fully returned.

Studying for comps at The Country Place or in Athens didn't really matter, the content and subject matter filled every cranny of brain matter, with all waking minutes full of recalling some communicative principle, some tidbit of esoteric knowledge, and even every sleeping moment was haunted with dreams of the same. One could not escape. So when Rick came by my office late one eve and said it was time for a break, to go view bare-breasted babes of celluloid and drink a beer, my answer was a hearty and quick, "Make mine a Rolling Rock!"

126

Off we trudged up a little alley next to Kantner Hall that leads conveniently to Court Street, viaduct for beer and pizza joints, party central to many a Bobcat (the mascot of OU), night time home to coed hotties, all seeking the flowing taps of liquid hop-infused libations. 'Twas a genius the one who invented small college towns. Down the quiet little alley we walked, with Court Street sounding like a Mardi Gras parade down St. Charles Street in New Orleans. Rick and I wondered what the heck all the commotion was. Through the sidewalk and street party maze we ended up at The Athena for Wednesday midnight skin-flicks, of course, in the support of the arts. An hour and a half later, Marilyn Chambers still fresh in our heads, we had not put a half sole of shoe on the sidewalk just out of the theater, when we saw students scattered in the middle of the street. Off to our right were Athens' Finest, fully garbed in riot gear, shields, guns, and what I would learn were "knee-knockers," a sawed off shotgun that shoots pellets on the ground and stings enough to cause the retreat of even the most recalcitrant, justice-possessed, or drunk student. They sounded like sandblasting against glass. Some students were throwing found objects, mostly beer bottles or stuff retrieved from trash barrels, and Rick and I stood speechless right there in the midst of a full blown college campus riot, wondering what was transpiring before our very eyes. About that time the riot cops reached us, and one guy, now not more than a few feet from us, yelled, "Get the fuck out of here you guys." Without a word, Rick and I hurriedly walked the half block, turned back down the alley and walked away from the Moore Russell Building, 1887.

"I don't need any part of that action," Rick said.

"What the hell are they protesting?" I asked.

"I don't think it's political, just a bunch a drunken, hormonal spring-crazed undergraduates."

"Sad day one can't take a leisurely stroll uptown and sip a beer. I wonder if the bagel buggy is still roasting up some hard donuts?"

Athens was known for its riots. A few years before, around the time of Kent State, the protesting in Athens that springtime shut down the campus, literally. Students were sent home, the semester was not completed, grades were assigned at that moment in time because finals did not happen, and students, faculty, administrators, and even townspeople, all received the monkey wrench treatment in their lives. There were some students that never came back in fall, hundreds that never wore caps and gowns, still others, many who were probably thankful, did not have to take a final exam. It got less press than the killings at Kent State up the road, but no

Ohio college campus, and arguably no other U.S. college, experienced more disruptive riots than the sleepy little Appalachian college town of Athens, Ohio. But all that was in the past, and my present focused only on a hot bagel covered with goo. The Bagel Wagon or Buggy, an Athens institution, served as a First Aid wagon on the corner of Union and Court providing mostly drunk students sustenance after a night on the town. I am sure the bagels soaked up alcohol and saved many a life, but beyond that, roasted bagels on a charcoal fire, slathered with your choice of cream cheese, butter, jams, peanut butter, and other treats just could not be beat under any condition. Legend from reputable sources reported, years later, that the Bagel Wagon entrepreneur became a millionaire and retired in his thirties. Maybe a college education is overrated.

Not needing knee-knockers, jail time, a riot without a cause, personal injury, confrontation with police, or other such nonsense, I resumed my obsessive studying, slowly working my way through the stacks of books, filling up notebooks with cogent points and needed information, and preparing myself to face the most daunting task of my academic life: taking sixteen hours of written comps, and suffering through two hours of oral examination with four profs trying to get my goat. This was the time I should have been stopping to smell the flowers, which were emerging as the harbingers of spring. This was the time when a young man's fancy should have been turning to love (or at least sex), but, instead, I hunkered down and got smart. That's when I met Abby.

Chapter15: Abby

You remind me
How sweet it all can be
How to whisper, how to sing
Of the passion we brought to everything
Of the promise that was spring
You remind me love is nothing
But the best that life can bring

You remind me of shooting stars
Life was a joy, it the living was hard
Rewards were few, and patience thin
Still it was easy to start all over again.
      (Robert Hunter, "You Remind Me")

All work and no play was making Scoop crazy. Abby waltzed in from the Sociology Department to take an INCO class in organizational development. It was spring. The air was clean, the sky was blue, the birds were chirping, the trees were in full leaf, the beer was flowing at the student union, and there were scantily-clad coeds everywhere. Cathy, Ben, and I, along with our new classmate Abby, were sitting on the famous deck overlooking the sidewalk of Tracy fame discussing the papers we needed to write. With the sun shining on us all, I could not help but be smitten with Abby. She was a little older, tall, long-legged, rosy cheeked, slender with slightly stooped shoulders and closely-cropped hair. She wore a hippie skirt, peasant blouse, and sandals. She had a classic face of beauty and intensity that radiated her bright intellect.

She spoke with authority, a soft certainty, a smooth determination of someone who knew herself. She was curious about others, but not the least bit shy to speak her mind. Strong women are always very sexy to me. Abby was all woman, and a strong one. She loved the country, had worked on a farm, and I would soon find out, had built her own cabin on a friend's property in Eastern Ohio. We ordered some pizzas and wiled away the afternoon. After a while Ben wandered off to home and Cathy left to meet friends.

"You want to go study at the library?" Abby asked.

"Sure," I calmly replied, thinking about obligations in the country. "Let me get my roommate to feed the animals and I'll join you on the second floor study stalls."

"See you over there, then," Abby said.

I made a quick trip next door to Dick's office, secured his agreement to take care of the menagerie of animals, and headed across the central green to the library for a fateful rendezvous. After a few hours of real study, and a little studying of Abby on my own, it was unspoken, but assumed, that we would head down to the Tavern for a beer or two. The conversation wound around our class, social issues, her studies, her application to Ph.D. programs, our love of the country, the Varmits, her debutante background and metamorphosis into radical feminist, and what we liked and disliked in others of the opposite sex. It was scintillating, easy, fun, comfortable, and well, I had never met a woman like this. She was not just an object of desire. She was an intellectual peer; more a curiosity and fascination than just another conquest. She admitted that she had been curious about me as well. She had observed how Ben and Cathy interacted with me, and she had listened to what they had said about me in other conversations to which I was not privy.

"I just wanted to find out why they liked you so," she admitted after a few beers.

Now I had other girls and women hot for me before, but this was different. I was interested in her as well.

"You like to smoke dope?" she asked.

"Yea, I've been known to light up a joint or two in my time," I smirked.

"My place is just around the corner. You want to go try this weed I got?" she intoned as she placed her hand on my forearm, a sign I was beginning to recognize and like.

Her apartment was upstairs in an old frame house common in Athens and so often used for student housing. It showed the wear and tear of years of youthful parties and inappropriate behaviors. She pulled out a small tray of weed, rolled up a joint, and passed it over to me. With lighter in hand, we torched a doobie and quietly enjoyed the aromas and mellowness of a good smoke. She played some cool jazz and we talked, immersed in the wonderful haze of an altered state of consciousness. Then she asked if I wanted to stay the night.

"That would be great, it's a long way to the country," I tried to say with coolness.

She briefly disappeared and returned hauling a futon mattress. She plopped it down in the middle of the living room, moved the coffee table out of the way, and threw some clean sheets on the bed.

"Does this work for you?" she asked.

"That'll do," I responded, not quite knowing who would be sleeping where except the instructions clearly indicated I was to crash here.

"I'll be back in a minute," she whispered, exiting the room.

I pruned down to my undies and T-shirt, wrapped my contact lenses in a tissue, put them safely on the coffee table, and crawled into bed. Abby reentered in a long, flannel gown, and snuggled into bed next to me. I had no earthly idea what to do with this woman. My mind was racing with conflicting notions and my heart was quickening next to a long and luscious body. Yet somehow I knew this woman was not like others, and my traditions and experience did not serve me well. We snuggled softly and quietly, I, not knowing what to say and she, I think, just waiting. Spooning behind her with my hand around her waist, I fell asleep to the intoxicating smells of a women's body, a room of dope smoke, and clean sheets. She, I assumed, fell asleep to her dreams.

It was a deep and seemingly endless sleep, although at first light we spontaneously awakened. She leaned over and kissed me on the lips. Already a good ways toward the classic and youthful morning hard-on, I put my hand behind her head and my other hand low around her waist and returned the kiss. These were kisses sweeter than wine, for sure.

My hand softly eased itself under her flannel night shirt and worked it up over her head. She deftly removed my T-shirt and now naked we began embracing passionately. She spoke quietly of contraception, and she climbed aboard and rode the magic wand to La La Land. Her body was lean and curvaceous, her breasts were small but perfectly proportioned, and the indentation of her waist suggested the curve of sensuality. It was a morning to remember. Abby was not just a passive receiver of joy. This beauty was rather an active giver of passion, an enjoyer of touch and tongue. This was qualitatively and quantitatively a different sexual experience. What was it, I wondered? Was it her age, her experience, her liberation? She exuded a feminine manliness of power, passion, and primacy.

We lay there for a while, and she questioned why we had not done it the previous night. I mumbo-jumbo-ed some notion that connection knows its own time, and it must have meant something, for she rolled over on me and kissed me again. Then she sat up and said she must get to class.

"Would you like to see The Country Place this weekend?" I bravely asked.

"I have some studying to get done and a concert Friday night, but if we can plan on booking it some, how about Saturday morning for the weekend?" she spoke like she was thinking out loud.

"I'll leave you a map before I go," I assured her.

Off she headed to the bathroom, my eyes following every step. I was mesmerized by every twitch of muscle, jiggle of ass, bounce of boobs. I lay there surrounded by the aromas of sex, semen, sheets, stale smoke, and satisfaction. With a deep breath, I restored my life back to reality and headed to class and comps, calling me ever so loudly amidst the residuals of foreplay and fucking. With a few days to prepare and a charming weekend with Abby behind me (some actual studying did get accomplished), I did not see or talk with anyone for a full week.

Chapter 16: The Passage Ritual

In the student newspaper that morning was this classified ad:

The time of reckoning had arrived. I picked up the prepared questions from the INCO secretary and walled up behind the door of my little grad student cubicle, basically a 3 x 4' closet. No books or props were allowed. It was mostly an honor system. With anticipation and trepidation I opened the packet of questions. It immediately became clear that each professor had put significant effort into tailoring questions to my specific studies. They intended to stretch my thinking and cover material that would be testament to the fact I had indeed mastered the subject matter. In fact, the word "mastered" had arisen in conversation with each professor in the days immediately preceding the time for comps. Stressing "mastering the material" must be part of the hazing ritual. For four days, I tried to eat well and sleep well, like I was in training for a sports event. I focused on nothing else but taking comps. As an undergraduate philosophy major at TCU, I found that long essay exams were the norm and I set Dr. Ferre's record for taking the longest time to complete an exam, gaining a reputation while subsequently acing the course. Give me the chance to write, to bullshit a little, and there is a fighting chance for me. Give me a multiple choice exam and expect me to pick A through E for the right answer is the kiss of death. Stimulation to the human species can come in myriad ways, from little kids spinning around to get a little high to the endorphins generated after a good run or a game of basketball to self-medication via drugs, to winning elections and awards. We like to have altered states of consciousness whether they are good for us or not. Of course, there are junkies out there. There are drugs, sex, money, winning, and a bunch of other addictions. Taking comps was my temporary addiction; it was a high, literally. Never before, and really never since, has my brain been so stimulated and active, so pure in memory, so clean in recall, so just jam-packed with information—such a finely honed organ. If my dick could have thought like my brain at that moment in time, I would have definitely considered making a living as a sexual athlete, without dwelling on the finer points of how I might work that out.

I wrote and wrote and wrote; I quoted long passages of pertinent matter; I used inductive logic to relate specifics to general principles and deductive logic to drill down from overarching theories to their manifestations in very particular events in human nature, communicative behavior, or generally recognized therapeutic interventions. I even knew page numbers of passages from the stack of books by the dining room table next to the big wood stove. On Friday afternoon, I turned in the last piece, walked out into the sunlight on the steps of Kantner Hall, and had no idea what to do with the rest of my life. I didn't know where I should walk or what I should do, and never even wondered where Tracy or Miriam or Abby were at that moment in my life. It was the culmination of all things academic I had achieved, participated in, or ever been a part of. But it was more.

It was a statement of who I was, how big my brain was, and how much I knew. It was a test of will, certainly, but also of capacity and capability. It was a very big test! I was on the free throw line with no time remaining, staring at the basket and two free throws, one to tie, two to win, and I just launched the ball skyward in confidence.

The difference, of course, is that the result of the free throw is known in an instant. Those of us who have played basketball extensively get a feeling as soon as the ball leaves our finger-tips. "It's going in, it's going in!" Or, "oh shit!" And we are usually right. But the comprehensive process takes longer than a free throw and gives no instant feedback. The professors needed more than a week to review my responses and to use them as a springboard to write follow up questions for my orals. Only then could they determine my readiness to become a Ph.D. candidate. Maybe ending the war, alleviating poverty, removing racism from the hearts of humans, or organizing environmental clean-ups, or sundry other worthy causes should have commanded my passion and attention, but pursuing a Ph.D. was my life at that moment, so the great causes would have to wait. I had another free throw to shoot: a two-hour oral exam.

The exam, scheduled about ten days hence, took place in the "living room" of Kantner Hall, with cozy chairs and couches, red colonial walls, and the architecture of what our forefathers found around them while writing the Constitution. It was the very room that hosted the very first get-together of new INCO students where I met Rick, Ben, and most all my colleagues-to-be for the next few years, some of whom were also taking comps at this time as well. I dressed up that day in my Sunday-go-to-meetin' finest: white shirt, suit, red dress tie, and shiny leather shoes with dark socks. I hadn't looked like this in many months. It was a professionally cordial affair, shaking hands and greetings all around. My major prof offered me a chair like I was a special guest at a state dinner.

Did I know what to expect? Not in the least. Was I nervous? You bet! Had I cogitated the worst case scenario of having to rewrite some or all of my comps and go through another oral exam again? Millions of times! Was there any confidence in my bones? Sure, for I knew more than all of these guys on certain subjects, plus a lot of stuff in their areas of expertise as well. The problem was that I did not even come near to knowing all that they knew and they weren't about to ask me stuff that I knew and they didn't. Such is the passage ritual into the brotherhood of the hooded robes of academia.

What transpired in the next two hours is a blur. I do know that when I would quote chapter and verse to answer their questions and nail the answer precisely on the head, they would nod politely and proceed to ask a follow-up question about how this related to the cosmic nature of the universe, or other absurdly broad postulate. Then, as I would begin to articulate eloquently and wax profoundly on the nature of the universe, they would shift my focus and ask a minute drill-down question seeking verse and chapter, page number and cogent quote, and gossip about whom the author slept with besides his spouse. Or so it seemed. I played this game as a good sport and did my best to deduct and induct around the stratosphere, trying my damndest to put words to their requests and substance to their inquiries. Was this taking minutes, hours, days? Would I have a three-foot beard when this passage ritual was over? Am I even making any sense?

Sometime in the middle of this hot-seat event, one of the faculty members posed a question about which I knew nothing. I had no idea what the fuck he was talking about, much less a hint of evidence that might lead to even a bullshit answer in my brain that could exit my mouth as words. I paused, thinking I could ask a follow-up question that might clarify his inquiry, but blankness overcame me. It was a humbling spot. I was supposed to have all the answers, at least for that two-hour block. I took a deep breath, paused, looked back directly at the inquirer and softly said: "I have no idea what you are asking, nor certainly how to answer it. Forgive me, but I just don't know that."

There was a longer pause on the part of each professor, eye contact exchanged among them all, and slight smiles crossed their faces. Dr. W. broke the silence and said that there were just a few more questions they wished to ask. Something palatable transpired. The thick air became pure oxygen, the cloudy sky brightened, their non-verbal behavior shifted, the faces of my inquisitors softened, and I got more nervous. But glory be in the highest, the clouds opened up, the stone rolled away from the grave, the waters parted, the blind saw, the lame walked, the water turned into wine, and probably a few other miracles simultaneously took place at that very moment, but who was counting? The next questions were about what I planned to do on my dissertation, what career goals I had, and how I planned to put my academic accomplishments to use, all future oriented and personal. My orals had evolved into a chitchat session; the professors had become more concerned counselors rather that grand inquisitors.

"Well, our time together is up," Dr. W. proclaimed. "Ted, if you could go up to my office and wait there for a few minutes to give my colleagues and me a chance to debrief, I'll be up there in a minute."

So up the stairs I went. Every performer, whether musician, dancer, athlete, singer, skater, or Olympian has been there. It is that tense moment right after the performance but before the scores are posted, the names of the individuals who made the team have been tacked on the bulletin board, the judges have ruled, the scholarship has been offered, or the critics have penned their reviews. It is the moment of truth, as the cliché goes, but what on earth does that mean? The moment of truth is a culmination of many moments of truth, and falsehoods, and false starts, and mishaps, and mistakes, and hard learning, and lessons, and small steps and tiny victories, and huge leaps forward, and three steps back. Our lives are moments of truth, if we so choose. But there I sat in an empty office, hands clammy and sweaty, mind racing, body at attention for a few minutes more before possible collapse. "Just hold on," I thought. Was it minutes? Probably, but who knows? I was in a parallel universe where time did not exist. The door opened and Dr. W sat down in his desk chair and smiled, either sympathetically or exuberantly, I could not tell which.

"How did I do?" finally came out of my mouth.

"Well that is my question, exactly, of you; how do you think you did?" he reversed the question.

So I pontificated with the voice of authority for a while, saying something erudite I hope, but who knows? He kept probing, until finally I began discussing the question on which I was clueless. Again I repeated slowly and quietly with resignation: "I just don't know." After a long pause, Dr. W. softened his voice and said: "Congratulations, Ted, you have passed your comprehensive exams and are now a Ph.D. Candidate." He reached out and shook my hand.

He continued: "The committee thought you did exceptional work on your written exams, and each would like a session to go over them with you in the next couple of weeks. They also think your answers in the oral exam ranged from brilliant to pretty good, with a little BS thrown in for filler. But that is not why you passed. We passed you because the committee had agreed that if you said at some time during the oral exam that you just did not know something, and meant it, we would pass you. Your knowledge of the subjects is unquestionable; your perspective of yourself in relationship to knowledge was what we questioned and were unsure about."

I'm sure he meant to mention humility, self-deprecation, and other such nonsense of the humble variety, but I got the message. No pain, no gain. I was the only student that term that did not have to rewrite any comp questions, and I felt lucky, rewarded, and yes, humble, for what I had learned and accomplished.

I should have raced down the stairs and yelled and screamed and thrown papers in the air, but I quietly crept down the hall and encountered Cathy, who gave that look of empathy, curiosity, and tension.

"I passed," I said matter-of-factly, hugged her and continued silently out into the perfect spring Athens day, and wondered what to do with the rest of my life.

A few days later I did have the opportunity to talk at length with each committee member and the student/teacher relationship seemed insignificant and certainly changed. The irony is that in those post-comp conversations I learned more about myself and the epistemology of my life than at almost any other time. Dr. S., my guidance and counseling prof, asked me if I recalled what I had said to him on the day that I turned in my comp answers and he asked me how I thought I had done on a certain question. I had truthfully told him that I wasn't sure and that I was not certain I had nailed it like the others. Now he could tell me, "Ted, I had to reread that question four times before I scored it after you communicated to me that you had doubts about your answers because you set me up to look for difficulty, inadequacy, and possible failure. The first time I read it I was about to agree with your assessment of your answer, but something did not ring true. It was so much different than the other students' approach to the question that I just about wrote it off as weak. But something inside me said to read it again, and again, and again. I came to the conclusion that it was the most creative and unusual approach to that counseling methodology I had ever read. In fact, I am thinking about using your ideas and writing an article about them. So what is the lesson here for us?"

That one I had to think about. But then it dawned on me, and I said, "My perspective clouded yours, and I set you up to see the question a certain way and did not give you the chance to figure it out for yourself. Is that close?" I asked. He nodded. In hundreds of instances since then, I have tried to refrain, even as opinionated as I am, from not prejudging one's perspective ahead of judgment time. Whether consulting with a CEO, doing a wine or chocolate tasting or serving on a board of directors, that little bit of learning has served me well. I have no earthly idea now what the content of the question was back then, but I do remember that learning comes in many packages, and for those small presents, we should be grateful.

Chapter 17: The Pig Roast

> Hawk--I'll never forget all we've
> shared and done. May the years
> ahead bring you the best. Keep in
> touch. Indians over the Yankees.
> Willie.
>
> "J.J." Thanx for a great year,
> Clevelbush Here we come. "T."
>
> Dummy, You really do look sweet
> enough to eat. I'll miss you. Pillsbury
> Dough Boy.
>
> Bozo--For all the good times &
> Just for being you. Lots of
> love--Bitch.
>
> Tango "Turkey" Ted.--Wishing
> you sunshine for the Pig Roast and a
> Happy celebration to all--Chug.
>
> Suckwad and Fat Boy--You may
> to like snakes And you like to keep
> us awake. We know you need your
> toenails cut. And your hair's getting a
> bit too much but, We all can't be
> perfect can we, can we.....CAN WE!
> The Real Women.
>
> Darin, This has been the best 3
> years of my life. Thanks for being
> such a major part of it. Good Luck
> cutie. Stu.

Classes wound down, and two things consumed me: one an obligation, the other a celebration. At the last meeting of the Graduate Student Council I had been elected president of the previously mentioned august group, more by default than intention, and with less altruism than self advancement. Mickey and Anise would be returning from South America, and I needed a place to stay. The presidency came with a better stipend and a free apartment on the South Green. I could keep my connections to

Meigs County but be closer to campus and more dissertation-focused. The outgoing president was graduating and immediately heading to Europe, so the obligation of attending and speaking at the graduation ceremony that spring was transferred to me. I was expected to give a little three-minute speech to the graduate students at commencement, no big deal.

But first, I had a pig roast to plan. With invitations to fellow grad students, honored faculty, the dean, the Varmits, some neighbors, and a few out-of-town guests, the weekend before graduation ceremonies was dedicated to a giant party at The Country Place. With no urgent school obligations imminent and the ordeal of comps successfully behind me, it was time to party. It would not be my last but certainly my biggest blowout at The Country Place.

Mike, my buddy from TCU, with whom I had bonded when we, unknowingly, switched girlfriends and had to have a come-to-Jesus meeting to check signals and figure things out, flew into Columbus from Washington, DC. He worked at the Office of Management and Budget trying to make sense of the Federal budget and be civil to the demands of Henry Kissinger, literally. Captain Crunch, also a colleague of Mike's from our Horned Frog days, and I drove the eighty-eight miles to the airport and picked up a very tall and distinguished, double-breasted suited and fine silk tie-wearing, very ready to party bureaucrat. Just about Lancaster, we lit up a big doobie and within a few miles the spread sheets of financial data were far from Mike's mind. In fact, he was higher than kite, as the cliché goes. We passed a large field with rows and rows of four-foot stakes standing at attention about five feet apart.

"What are they growing there?" Mike inquisitively inquired.

"Oh, they're growing tomato stakes for gardeners," I said as straightforwardly as possible.

"No shit," he said slightly surprised. "I didn't know that's how they did it."

"Yea, Ohio is known for its tomato stakes, reputed to be the best around," I added britannically.

We sat silently for a slight while, and then the Captain and I just lost it, laughing so hard we had to stop the car by the side of the road. What Mike had failed to see were the little starts of tomato plants nestled near the stakes. But we got him, fodder for fun. This did not, of course, crush Mike's ego, a very bright Marshall Fellow, President of TCU's Student Government, an accomplished college debater, and fun-loving, guitar-playing rock 'n' roller. But it sure set the tone for the weekend.

Bob, the Varmit, had given me some leads on where to get a pig, as it turned out, down in South County from a farmer named Leo. So off we went to Leo's pig farm to bring a little piggy to market, or a roast as it were. Mike, Captain Crunch, Abby, and I cruised the hills and dales of Meigs County, and even with explicit instructions from both Bob and Leo, it was still heard, "Where the fuck is this place?" Fred, my turkey buddy, in the meantime, stayed back at The Country Place to hold down the fort. He was in for a long wait.

Getting there was harder than knowing when we had found it. A pig farm, let us just say, carries its own indelible signature of arrival. The barren hills, rutted and muddy, were not even the first sign of our destination, no. Pigs might be smarter than dogs and more trainable than other pets, but they still can create an assault on the olfactory senses far exceeding a dairy farm, a sheep ranch, a turkey facility, or acres of chicken coops. Pigs stink.

We met Leo and introduced ourselves. We finalized a price and approximate weight. Now it is not like these porkers are in a little barn and easy to get to; no, they have free range to roam and places to hide, and therefore we had acres to try to track down the perfect pig. Leo carried his rifle at his side, all of us had pounds of pig shit on our shoes, and the pigs, smarter than we were, just did not want to party with the fearless five-some. Leo said we'd sneak up on one. From my vantage point, there was no way in hell this strategy was going to work. I was reflecting upon the rooster shoot back at The Country Place where our taxpayer' money was wasted on Captain's marksmanship.

It was getting toward dusk and I was getting anxious. The pigs seemed to be getting smarter and Leo seemed to be getting dumber. My hopes of having a pig to roast were waning. Abby suggested that she and I go around the little rise where the pigs were congregating and quietly march them back to Leo and death, easier for us than the targeted pig. So off Abby and I trotted, pig shit and all. She sensed my anxiety and started to laugh, not at me but at the situation in which we found ourselves. Laughter is contagious, and soon both of us were laughing our asses off, to the curious wonderment of the others. Another amazing thing happened: the pigs came up to us, for they must have been a fun-loving breed after all. They actually followed us around. Now picture this: there were not just a few little piggies, there were upwards of eighty, many weighing lots more than I, and some twice as much as Abby. It was damn near dark now, and our chances of bagging a beast appeared next to impossible. At sixty feet,

I looked up at Leo who had shouldered his rifle, cocked the trigger, and aimed it right at us. He pulled the trigger, the shot rang out, and I feared that we were caught up in a Hitchcock movie, evil and death hung around us. I would have hit the ground but I didn't have time and I didn't want to wallow in pig shit. I jumped ten feet in the air and passed Abby heading up on the way down. My heart was pounding, my mind was mush, and pig shit splashed on my jeans. Yet, a mere five feet away, one perfectly-sized and quite pretty pig dropped to the ground with a squeal. Then silence. By Jove, I think he's got it. I unsheathed the knife I had borrowed from Mickey, reached down, and in one fell swoop, I cut its throat, grabbed its legs, pointed its head downhill, and watched as the blood drained rapidly from the pig's body. Leo, feeling quite proud and exuding confidence, Mike, and the Captain came rushing up about then, and we, as descendants of the hunters and gatherers, stood stoically above our bleeding prey.

"Nice shot," I said to Leo.

"Good knife," he returned the compliment.

Mike, the Captain, Abby, and I stashed the pig in an old blanket in the trunk of the car, not a small feat I might add, and headed off in the dark to The Country Place.

It was a reunion of epic proportion. Mickey and Anise had returned from the South having logged 18,000 miles in the Volvo, rebuilding the engine almost twice, and making it all the way to the extreme reaches of Patagonia. They were full of travel adventures and stories galore. They bragged of conducting pig roasts in their past, and here they were, visitors in their own home, doing it again. Mickey was lighting a fire under a fifty-five gallon metal drum, hoping to dip the whole hog in it and soften the hair enough to remove. Anise was in the kitchen preparing a stuffing of everything but the kitchen sink: honey, molasses, fruits, spices, onions, apples, and much, much more. It smelled of what I imagined a market bazaar in Turkey would smell like: exotic, spicy, citrusy, and sweet. Captain and Mike, strong of body and with instructions in mind, began digging the fire pit that would serve as our roasting "oven" for eighteen hours. What a scene.

Mickey gutted the pig and it was nothing like my nostrils had ever experienced. Pigs' guts makes one gag. Pure and simple, this smell could be used for aversion therapy in prison for sex offenders. When they were shown various erotic stimuli, the therapist would immediate spray the convicts with an awful concoction if their penises, already wired, showed slightest arousal. Upon inhaling, it would forever put the kybosh on them wanting to doodle little girls, or whatever their particular object of lust happened to be. Actually such therapists used a product of afterbirth and excrement, but I think that pig guts, which come with a built-in channel of crap, would do just as well. While I was gagging, Cranfield was ecstatic and intoxicated. Pig guts were just doggie treats for him. We saved the liver and heart, then tossed the pile of innards to an eager canine. He consumed the stinking guts with gusto. But who were we to judge? Within hours we humans would be doing the same, albeit to different parts of the swine.

We could not get enough hot water, by fire, by stove, by tap, or by God. Pig hair is deeply entrenched, and nothing we could do seemed to loosen it. We tried to scrape it off with hunting and kitchen knives, and we even tried shaving cream and razors, which kinda worked but was so laborious that it dulled the razors and we ran out. Finally, by midnight, we had the pig more or less hairless and we had crammed stuffing into every orifice. Meanwhile the Captain and Mike had finished digging a monster pit in the middle of the yard between the root cellar and the goose pen. Now Anise announced that it was time to marinate the pig in her concocted mash of all things sweet, savory, and spicy. It truly was an international pig, marinated with curry, chiles, honey from around the world, saffron, oregano, lemongrass, mint, and all assortment of pureed fruits blended together and ready to lather the pig. But where? The round watering trough was too small and really dirty. Then, someone suggested the bathtub. With Mickey grabbing a couple of legs and Fred the others, we toted that hog into the bathroom and plopped it right into the tub. Anise was thrilled. She quickly commenced rubbing the carcass with her massive ooze of marinade. With standing room only, the crew, crowded in a tiny country bathroom, stood there and admired our handy work. We were exhausted, yet proud, accomplished, and laughing. Even the dear pig seemed strangely contented. Later that morning we lowered the pig into the funeral pyre of its destiny, a sacred place that would become its final resting place as a whole hog.

Everyone in Meigs County claimed to be an expert on roasting pigs, like Texans with BBQ, Michiganders with ice fishing, and Alaskans with moose hunting. The word on the street, or the country road in this case, instructed the cookers to first heat some rocks and then place them in the pit to retain the temperature so the pig would cook more evenly and thoroughly. So our rock-gathering party, after many a reconnaissance to procure the perfect-sized stones, filled the bottom of the pit and we were ready to roast. Well, not quite yet. The rocks needed hours to heat, and we could not place the pig directly on the rock for the pig would commence to burn to a crisp. Discussion ensued as the ragged crew brainstormed myriad ways to suspend the carcass midway in the pit far from the hot rocks not to burn it while close enough to cook. In fact, I surmised, having the capacity to raise and lower the animal seemed critical to our culinary success. In the barn were some old refrigerator grates and plenty of fencing wire, so at 1:00 a.m., we rigged up a system of grates, wires, pulleys, and above-ground anchors that would suspend the pig exactly where we needed it in the pit of fire. Now all we needed was some wood split and stacked, ready to keep the heat up to temperature. At about 3:00 a.m., tired, wasted, sleepy, dirty, and cranky, but accomplished, we scheduled hourly visits by each of us to stoke the fire and heat the rocks so the pit would be ready to start cooking pork come daylight. Abby and I staggered up the stairs to bed exhausted and filthy. My duty came in a couple of hours, and before daybreak I tossed in a few more logs and watched the sparks rise from the pit to join the sparkling stars of the morning with a cool mist chilling my bones as it hovered in Copperhead Hollow.

"What the hell you boys been doing with yourselves?" Rick shouted loudly outside the house awaking all of us when sleep was all we wanted. Farm boys just do not understand the meaning of the sanctity of the morning. Worse than a bunch of roosters outside the door, Rick's wakeup call brought cat calls and groans. Somehow I stumbled down the stairs and glared.

Nonplussed, Rick declared: "You better get that pig on or it's not going to be done until Sunday!"

I fingered him to follow me and I led him to our supper, raw, cold, and ugly, lying peacefully in our bathtub marinade. A slight grin came over Rick's face. He motioned to pick up one end and we hauled the pig over to the pit. Rick placed his hand down about half way to check the heat.

"Not bad," he proclaimed. "We need to wrap this puppy in foil and put her in the pit. We probably have just enough time to get her done by suppertime."

While I retrieved the foil, Rick went around the side of the goose pen, got a big bucket and filled it with water. Then we gently put the pig on our wired grate mechanism and lowered it into the hot pit. Ricky eyed it silently.

"You think we're going to need some water to put out a fire flare-up?" I asked.

"No stupid, that's to soak the logs in so they don't burn up too fast and fuck up the pig," he condescended. Another country opinion added to the scores of others I was privy to in the past twenty-four hours.

144

"We're losing too much heat in this open pit," Rick worried aloud. "You got anything to cover this thing to keep the heat in?" he asked.

Now this was a conundrum. The pit was almost three feet wide and five feet long, and nothing burnable would work. Then it dawned on me and off I trotted without a word. In a few minutes, I returned from behind the barn hauling an old rusty hood of a car and clanged it down by the pit.

Rick smiled, "It's perfect."

We covered the pit with the car hood and it did fit perfectly. What a sight. Smoke gently rising from this hole in the ground covered with a humped metal auto part. I was beginning to feel quite Appalachian. Rick cooked that pig. He stood vigilant all day, adjusting the grate, soaking the wood, and placing the logs appropriately on the rocks to make sure that the heat stayed even while our supper slowly roasted to perfection. It was a damn good thing that Rick took over, for I had a thousand other distractions. There was food to prepare, tables to set up, place settings to arrange, much to clean, and Abby to hug and work alongside. Mike ditched his suit for jean shorts and a white T-shirt, a uniform he would live in for several more days until we dumped his tired ass back at the airport.

In the afternoon, Abby and I headed to the pond to clean up. With Dr. Bonner's peppermint soap in hand, we walked up the hill for a refreshing dip. From our vantage point above, The Country Place all looked spectacular. Dick loved to mow so the lawn looked great. He had used a hand trimmer and gone around the buildings, fences, and roads, meticulously edging the grass to perfection. Shortly after their arrival, Mickey and Anise had commented on the new energy and beauty of the place. Thanks to me, they felt more at home than when they'd left. I felt proud. After exactly one year, living in the country suited me, fulfilled me, caused my heart to soar like a hawk, and made me feel at home. After our pause to take in the view, Abby and I stripped and eased into the pond, borrowing an air mattress that someone had left floating around aimlessly. She climbed on and floated around aimlessly herself. I swam up and blew on her tummy. We wrestled for supremacy of mattress and ended up sitting on it together straddling it like a horse while facing each other. By weight, gravity, and maybe desire, our bodies crunched together and our crotches united. We looked longingly at each other, and my now erect dick slid into her as we balanced on the mattress as one. The water supported us, the mattress suspended us, the bounce of the motion excited us, and the sun warmed our upper bodies. What a ride!

I have never looked at air mattresses the same since. In fact, the smell of peppermint, prevalent in Dr. Bronner's PURE CASTILE SOAP, has elicited notions of the erotic ever since. Her head tilted back in ecstasy, I tried not to yell anything, and we broke out in uncontrollable giggle. We were still tired, but now we were clean and invigorated. Guests would be arriving soon, so wrapped in towels we strolled down the hill to dress and get ready to party.

A year of living large in the country, a reuniting with the house owners returned from their travels, a reunion with old friends from TCU, a fascinating woman as friend and lover, and a celebration of more than just passing comps; it was a confluence of my life all around me. Rick was dutifully tending the roasting pig, Mickey and Anise were readying the serving dishes and tables, and I wandered around not knowing what to do except be appreciative of all of those acts. Just then, I heard loud music coming from the little parking lot down the hill, soon followed by the distinctive sound of pick-up truck doors slamming shut. The Varmits had arrived. A procession of them appeared from the forest and emerged onto the sweeping lawn manicured by Dick. They carried cases of beer on their heads, cradled potluck dishes, nestled jugs of wine under each arm, and, of course, had shirt pockets brimming with doobies. There was no doubt that they were ready to party. Surprise! Soon thereafter a mix of fellow grad students, professors, and a dean or two gingerly trudged up the road not really knowing what to expect. They were dressed for city partying, so the contrast between the spit-and-polished university types and the unwashed and scraggly Varmits clashed before our very eyes. Colliding cultures, for sure. This gathering was testament to the bipolar nature of my existence with successful academic types and social degenerates from the hills around me.

With the assorted crowd now gathered around the pit, we pulled the pig up and removed the foil from its body. Someone yelled we needed to put an apple in its mouth for full effect. Abby ran into the kitchen and procured the traditional red fruit. Now we were officially ready to pig out, and we did, big time. Naturally, the Varmits surged to the front of the line and went immediately for the loin running down each side of the backbone. Luckily the more polite pillars of academia thought the ham was the prize cut so all were happy. The feast of potluck dishes seemed endless. Homemade pies and cakes abounded on the dessert table, and the coolers of beer were constantly visited throughout the evening. Abby and I stood by holding hands and surveying the scene and chuckling, for she too had lived among ne'er-do-wells in the country before spending time at the university. We viewed the contrast of clothes, life styles, expressions, eating and drinking habits, education, interests, life choices, companions, and a myriad of other opposites with amusement and anthropological detachment.

Bob, the Varmit, brought over a beer and joint and handed them to me. "OK, Bob, what do you want from me?" I asked.

"Just a great party, Scoop. Why would you think something else?" he said.

Beer was sipped, joints were passed back and forth, and finally Bob confessed.

"Scoop, we want to sponsor a Varmit softball tournament this summer in Athens, you know, like the one we won last summer."

"Great idea. That was fun. Do we get to play in our own tournament?" I asked.

"Probably not. We should be able to get about sixteen regional teams, many that played last summer, and hopefully we can rent the fields there in Athens along the Hocking."

"When do you plan on having this extravaganza?" I inquired.

"Late July, early August looks about right. But one other thing, Scoop. You know the Varmits, we ain't much for organizing anything, hell, not even our own lives. You got the brains and organizational skill we need to run this thing. You think you could be our lead organizer? Now, I can help you get the teams signed up; we got the list of all the softball teams in the area and contact info, and all of us Varmits would help, but, man, we need some smarts to coordinate all the shit that has to happen."

Flattery can be a fine persuader, and I immediately thought about the disaster a tourney run by the Varmits could be, a fiasco of laughable proportions. A little summertime distraction from the dissertation proposal writing would be well-deserved, and this was right up my alley, or down my base path, or whatever, so I said, "Yes."

"Bob, if you think everyone will pitch in and help, I'll run a softball tourney this summer. The First Annual Varmit Invitational Softball Tournament. How does that sound?"

Bob raised his beer in a toast, and with a clink of the can I became the director of the tourney-to-be. Little did I know what I was getting into.

By the time midnight rolled around, the last remaining partiers had stumbled down the hill. Mike, Abby, and I stood in the kitchen with the residual mess, passed the final doobie around, and reflected on pulling off such a magnificent party. We told the story of the great pig kill with Leo and his trusty rifle. Finally Abby and I trudged up the stairs to bed, extremely tired hombres ready to get naked and sleep without care.

For months, the pig roast would be a topic of conversation among my university colleagues, with them often reporting: "I had such a great conversation with one of those, what do you call them?" and I'd add, "Varmits." And the Varmits would talk about how shocked some of those same academics were when they discovered that a Varmit could actually put together a proper English sentence.

Chapter 18: Eric Sevareid and
Three Minutes of Fame

Ohio University's commencement ceremony took place in the big round arena where the Bobcats played bad basketball. As president of the Graduate Student Council, all I had to do was give a short speech addressed mainly to the graduating masters and doctoral folks, but another 8000 or so undergraduates, parents, siblings, cousins, aunts and uncles, grandparents, friends, and assorted associates would also be privy to my words. It was only to be three-minutes long, but I did not take it lightly. I represented the School of Interpersonal Communication and the Graduate Student Council. In addition, I felt a responsibility to thousands of undergraduate public speaking students that had graced my classroom. As a speech TA, I had listened to their five speeches per quarter and given them oral and written critiques. Of the hundreds of speeches I evaluated,

I can only remember three, and not for their content. One was a poor, scared girl from a small, dusty Kansas farm. Midway through her speech I saw her eyes roll back in her head, and, like a tree being cut in the forest, she toppled and hit her head with a crack and a bounce before I could get my butt down the aisle to catch her. Fortunately, she survived. In another instance a young man spoke about martial arts and used a classmate to demonstrate some karate moves, miscalculated and caught his friend across the face causing massive quantities of blood to begin squirting throughout the classroom. The unlucky kid still has a scar to this day to prove his story. The third one was a returning soldier from Vietnam that talked about losing a buddy in combat. The whole class was in tears. I hoped to avoid such catastrophes.

For every one minute of the speech, I prepared about five hours, a ridiculous ratio. But if I had learned anything from my own teaching, I knew that preparation is key to oratorical greatness. I typed out the speech on 3 x 5-inch cards, double spaced with notations for pauses, emphases, pace, intensity, and rate. Adorned in my Sunday-go-to-meetin' dark suit, white shirt, shiny shoes, and best tie, I reported as instructed to the tunnel from where the hapless hoopsters of Ohio would enter the sparsely-populated arena for home games. There lined up were the President of the University, the Dean of the Graduate School, the Faculty Senate President, the undergraduate speaker, the local minister who would invocate, the registrar's office representatives who would pass out the diplomas, the featured speaker, and me. Hands were shaken all around, final processional instructions and seating arrangements given, and we nervously awaited the orchestration to begin. All of this pomp and circumstance took time and a little drudgery, only punctuated by the unseemly shrieks of family members when they first caught a glimpse of their graduating loved one. The organizer motioned us to begin, and we moved out in unison to take our positions on the stage. Oh my goodness, this was no basketball game. The place was packed, standing room only. The graduates filled the floor, every seat was occupied, the aisles overflowed as if in a Fire Marshall's nightmare, and people were waiting in the outer foyer to get into the arena. It was a passage ritual not to be missed, the most coveted ticket in town. There were typical nice-nice welcomes by the president and the dean, an invocation by the minister, and a short speech by the undergraduate student council president. It was a sophomoric, inane, piss-ant presentation that would barely have merited a passing grade in my public speaking class. Now it was my turn. Who knows what to expect when first speaking before an arena full of people, most of whom are more ready to celebrate than to sit and listen?

I confidently strode to the podium and paused to gaze at the masses. I wanted my first line to grab their attention, so I had worked a long time perfecting what I hoped would be captivating. It was. The place fell deadly silent, and you could have heard an ant fart in the corner of the arena. I began my little story about how a graduate student was traveling in a far country and met an old man by the side of the road and asked the old man what kind of people live in yonder village. The old man asked what kind of people did he come from, and the OU grad says: "fools, vagabonds, and cheats." The old man simply stated, "You'll find the people there the same." The place was still quiet, and I felt a powerful surge in my inner being, for ears and eyes of thousands focused their attention and interest on me and the sensation was unique in my life. It was later that I thought of the power of speech and how it has been used for good and evil and how intoxicating it could be in the voice of Hitler or Roosevelt or Gandhi or Napoleon. Not that the analogy put me anywhere near their league, but the feeling, the quintessential human experience of power, must be understood as a narcotic and intoxicant of life. I continued the speech by telling of another student meeting the same old man by the side of the road and asked the same question. But this student told the old man that the people from where he came from were true, just, and good. The elderly sage smiled and advised: "You'll find the village people there the same." My voice inflection rose toward the end of the speech, my words each enunciated distinctly, slowly with more breath support I closed my speech right at three minutes and paused. The cheers were deafening, I think even a few in the audience stood. I knew it was a knockout punch, and I smiled slightly as I, yes, proudly, stepped back to my seat.

After the ceremony, Dean W., a tired old man who headed the College of Communication, moved to the podium to introduce his old friend, Eric Sevareid, the featured speaker. They had served together as World War II correspondents and continued a respectful relationship over the years. Mr. Sevareid was nearing retirement from CBS News. The protégé of Edward R. Morrow and the predecessor to colleagues Huntley and Brinkley, he was the trusted news voice for millions of Americans then serving in his last few years as a commentator on Walter Cronkite's evening news. The recipient of Emmy and Peabody Awards, Sevareid even portrayed himself in the movie *The Right Stuff*. The tall North Dakota native of Norwegian ancestry spent lots of time in most every American's living room, so this audience knew who stood before them, and he carried high credibility. The distinguished journalist delivered a safe speech: not boring, a little traditional, full of platitudes, but not embarrassing. The audience was antsy to see their loved ones actually graduate, and Sevareid stood in the way of the main ceremonial purpose. The applause was polite, not rousing.

The time had come. Names were called, cheers were scattered throughout the arena, and it looked like a thousand other high school and college graduation events carried out in cities and hamlets across the country. When the president announced the shifting of the tassel, hats were thrown into the air and loud cheers ensured. The recessional led us out into the sunny day.

The podium party was invited to a reception at the president's home located on a lovely short street on the edge of the university only a block from the central green and the administration building. It had a glassed garden room off to one side, pillars of grandeur on the front porch, fine wood paneling, and trim and royal staircases befitting the titular head of a 16,000 enrollment university. The catered food most interested me, for it had been hours since sustenance, and grazing the buffet of goodies was my focus. "Varmits," I thought, "eat your heart out." They could have made short work of the spread before me. I retired to the garden room to stuff my face, nicely of course, like my mother taught.

I looked up and saw Mr. Sevareid walking purposefully across the room with plate in hand, coming directly toward me. I looked around me to spot whom he might be heading for but there was no one near. He walked up to me, stuck out his right hand, and said, "Young man, you said more in three minutes than I did in twenty."

He seemed to tower over me, such a tall and famous man, made small by the television sets of his day. But here he was, the face of the evening news right before me, an interviewer of presidents and other heads of state, seeking me out to offer a congratulatory comment. I swallowed hard, and I think that I managed to utter an audible "thank you," even adding "Mr. Sevareid." He launched into a dialogue about how he really didn't like parties and social events like this, and we chatted, like colleagues, for a few minutes before some fame-seeking old ladies came up to gush over the celebrity in our midst. With a parting "good job and all my best to you," directed my way, he let himself be whisked away to do what he seemed to hate: chitchat at social events. But somehow I felt like he had briefly blessed me with a real moment with the real person behind the TV lights and broadcasts. He just seemed like a shy fellow from North

Dakota, resembling any number of humble farm folks I grew up knowing in the prairies of the Midwest. It was a supreme compliment, and one I have cherished for decades. As America mourned his passing in the early nineties, I probably paused just a little longer in silence and appreciation for my three minutes with the man.

Chapter 19: The Road Trip to Revelation

Truckin'—got my chips cashed in
Keep truckin'—like a doodah man
Together—more or less in line
Just keep truckin' on.

Most of the cats you meet on the street speak of true love
Most of the time they're sittin' and cryin' at home
One of these days they know they gotta get goin'
out of the door and down to the street all alone

Truckin'—like a doodah man
Once told me you got to play your hand
sometime—the cards ain't worth a dime
if you don't lay 'em down

Sometimes the light's all shining on me
Other times I can barely see
Lately it occurs to me
What a long strange trip it's been

Truckin'—I'm goin' home
Whoa-oh, baby, where I belong
Back home—sit down and patch my bones
and get back truckin' on
        (Robert Hunter, Jerry Garcia, Phil Lesh, and Bob Weir, "Truckin'")

The next week gave me a chance to take a collective breath. With classes behind me, comps done, my public speaking obligation a success, and a year to write a dissertation ahead, what could be a better way to unwind from the rigors of academia than a road trip with a beautiful woman? Somehow Abby and I concocted and conceived cranking up her old VW van and hitting the road. The van was an icon of the era, pure white with a noisy and underpowered engine. It wasn't technically a camper but it was outfitted for the road with a mattress to sleep on and a cooler for beer and other road staples. We fancied ourselves with the likes of Jack Kerouac, the Merry Pranksters of Ken Kesey's Kool-Aid Acid Test gang and his psychedelic bus "Furthur," John Steinbeck and his dog Charley, and other road-worthy literary travelling figures. It was time to go see "Maerka," the pronunciation of "America" by those who lived in the locales of our itinerary. Points of destination included New Orleans, a city both of us loved and where we had free lodging at my sister's house. Then onto Oklahoma City where I grew up and where my parents lived. On the way back we planned a stop in Bloomington, Indiana to check out the university where Abby would soon matriculate. She wanted to check it out and meet her soon-to-be professors. We had a target date of returning to Athens on my birthday in late July. With a couple of ounces of good pot, the cooler loaded with goodies, Abby in an ankle-length skirt, peasant blouse, and sandals, me in shorts and T-shirt, we climbed into the fuck-mobile of the era and headed out Highway 50, leaving Meigs County behind, into Vinton County and points beyond.

In days of old before steamships plied western waters, many a flat-bed boat floated down the Ohio River to the Mississippi ending in the Crescent City. Laden with Midwestern grain, the flat-bed boats floated easily downstream with the flow. But the northbound traffic upstream was relegated to cumbersome keelboats or an overland passage, by foot or horse-drawn wagon. The route followed the trails of ancient animals and peoples, some of the meandering curves carved out by bison heading north to the salt licks of the Cumberland Plateau from the grazing plains of the Mississippi Valley. Supply stations, waysides, blacksmiths, and other entrepreneurs set up shop along what became known as the Natchez Trace. Boatman trudged toward home and wagons brought valuable finished goods to the maturing farms and villages of the Ohio Valley. When Abby and I entered the Trace in Kentucky, we became tourists of a National Park of 454 miles of scenic byway, connecting, not literally but by practice, the far reaches of Pittsburgh to the Mississippi Delta, through Ohio, Kentucky, Tennessee, Alabama, and Mississippi. Restoration of the Natchez Trace into a historic automobile road was a New Deal project during the Great Depression, involving the CCC and other agencies. It was sanctioned as a National Park in 1938. This beat the hell out of freeways. We saw and hiked old trails used by the buffalo and Indians, stopped at refreshing waysides, passed miles and miles of forested land, fenced roadways, cypress swamps, and kudzu, the insidious and ubiquitous vine imported for soil erosion early in the twentieth century but now the scourge of the South. Known locally as the "foot-a-night vine," the "mile-a-minute vine," the "vine that ate the South," it engulfs whole trees, choking the life out of them, and relentlessly grabbing a hold of anything in its path. Abby and I, cruising along, watched in awe its power and pervasiveness. We visited Nashville for some good Southern cooking and camped out in the van. It was hot and humid when we reached New Orleans. Abby, with anthropology studies in her background, hit it off with my sister, an anthropologist by training and a teacher and writer extraordinaire. We slurped oysters at Felix's Oyster Bar, ate beignets and drank chicory and coffee mixed with cream in the wee hours of the morning at Café Du Monde, and wolfed down a couple of po' boys from a local Garden District purveyor of the classic New Orleans sandwich. A few days later we drove out of Louisiana through the northeast corner of the great state of Texas, and arrived in Oklahoma City to visit my folks.

Along the highways and byways of the South we dialed the radio for local music and naturally found mostly country and gospel stations. Though at first surprised, Abby soon tired of me knowing all the lyrics to both types of music. At one point, we left the needle for a while on a Christian Evangelical program of one Reverend Jones. He ranted and raved about his little booklet that would help fat people lose weight, and, of course, that meant a great percentage of his listening audience.

"Now folks, send me $5.00, or more to do the Lord's work, and I'll send you my sure-fire method to shed those extra pounds you're carrying around. The Lord says your body is the temple of God and you need to shape it up. But just the other day a lady calls me and says, 'Reverend Jones, I am way too skinny, and I need to gain weight, and bless the Lord, I don't know what to do.' So I say to her, send me your hard-earned cash and I'll send you the book and it will help you *gain* weight. For holy mercies, God goes both ways!"

"God goes both ways?" Abby repeated.

"Praise the Lord, he goes both ways." I said. And we commenced to get hysterical. The van careened around the highway, tears filled our eyes, and finally she pulled over on the shoulder so we could try to catch our breath. "God goes both ways" became a mantra in our relationship for many an excuse or reason for or against something. A supreme being so flexible, so willing to be open to the yin and yang of cosmic needs, seems somehow more reassuring, I have often pondered, than an almighty rigidly meting out commandments, edicts, and judgments. Either way, a bunch of five-dollar contributions here and there soon becomes real money; ca-ching, ca-ching for Rev. Jones.

Of course my parents loved me, but it was not without a slight bit of consternation that they were always trying to figure out if this one was the ONE. They needed me to have a long-term girlfriend, an engagement, and the prospect of a wedding and grandkids to be totally secure. My revolving door of girlfriends just did not fit the bill for them. Sleeping together before marriage in our house was always taboo, so Abby took my old room and I was out-posted to my brother's room that Daddy had carved out of half the garage for his last few years of high school. It had a wall heater but no air-conditioning, and it was July in Oklahoma. But I had been for a year hardened by the attic at The Country Place, so with a fan blowing hot air all night, sleeping was not a problem.

Abby found my boyhood stomping grounds quite invigorating. She seemed to fall in love with a little boy in his childhood home. She even seemed to be sexually stimulated by the situation surrounding my quasi-disapproving parents. So she wanted to make out in the TV room after the folks retired to bed, although I feared that Mom would come into the kitchen for her pills and there we would be, clothes askew, scrambling to appear fit for public decorum. So I escorted Abby out to Hugh's old bedroom, and we got it on even though the fan provided cooling in the low 90s. Sweat poured off our shiny bodies, and we spent hours in passionate orgy. This time, I knew it was hours for Abby commented on staying power.

The next night after a tour of Route 66, my high school, the local BBQ joint, and the National Cowboy Hall of Fame, we had supper with my mom and dad. Sensual Abby decided that she wanted to see where I used to go to make out with chicks from high school. Most of that activity had been carried on in cars on the short trips from church to the pizza parlor after youth fellowship meetings, but one spot I recalled did have romantic appeal, although, frankly, I probably had been there only once in my life for teenage petting. The shores of Lake Overholster, or Lake "Hold-her-closer" as we affectionately called the reservoir, was dotted with little camp-sites in the woods that offered seclusion and the promise of pussy. So off we went as twenty-somethings feeling like teenagers in my father's Buick. We drove the few miles to the lake and found a campsite far from the beaten path. Abby, surprisingly eager for quick sex, slipped off her panties from under her skirt and motioned me to slide over to the passenger side. With her skirt covering us, she straddled my loin and locked her wet pussy around my dick. I am sure that there were classmates who performed acts of togetherness similar to this when we were all in high school, but not me. I was a virgin into college, so making out and fucking in my father's car seemed surreal. But with two hands grasping ass cheeks and my hips gyrating to sensual bobbing, who could think or feel guilty or really care? We giggled and kissed and touched and cooed and snuck quietly into the house. Reluctantly, we separated to our respective bedrooms, having warranted a good night's sleep and targeting an early start the next morning heading to Indiana.

Somewhere around St. Louis, Abby decided that she needed some quiet time to focus and prepare for her interviews in Bloomington. For miles and miles, I read, drove, snoozed in the back of the van, and pretty much left her alone. By the time we reached the city limits of Bloomington, her mood had shifted somewhere far from any focus on me. We crashed at the house of a professor with whom she had become acquainted, and she communicated very clearly that I was in the way. She did not want me to meet anyone associated with her future life here, and she didn't want me to bother her as she made appointments and went about her business. It wasn't mean spirited, but she was direct and firm. I'm a mature person, and I certainly understood. But the contrast between being desired passionately for the past few days and then finding that she wanted me to vaporize and disappear so she could relax and be happy was simply disconcerting and hurtful to me. She had the power, which was a dramatic contrast to most of my relationships where I retained the power. My feeling of objectification hammered me with unknown emotions, nauseated my gut, and left my head spinning with self-doubt, diminished self-worth, and lessened self-hood.

Pain in love was not new; I had been madly in love with Patti when she was a freshman and I a sophomore. For one year we dated and wrote letters through the summer, and then she broke up with me fall term because she had met another guy in Austin that summer, and she didn't want to be tied down during her undergraduate years.

"If I could put you on a shelf for a few years and we then re-commission what we have had this past year, I would be for that," Patti consoled. The shelf life of love is short. It did not make me feel any better. As the old saying goes, there will be evil in the world as long as one cockroach is dying of unrequited love. Of course, romantic novels, even great novels, speak of soldiers off to war and back home awaits a true love to be reunited after plagues, war injuries, famine, rape, and other tragedies to make the story interesting. Humans just are not good at sitting on the shelf of life awaiting the love of their life to go out and have a good time. So I hustled her best friend, lamented she was not Patti, and got on with the rest of my life. Loss of love did hurt me at such a tender age. Patti and I feigned friendship for the next few years; she got married her senior year, and every time I saw her, my whole body and being would react with a tight tummy, a tied tongue, sweaty palms, and generic "flustration," a word my brother thought he invented.

But this loss of love with Abby was different from past ones; this feeling of powerlessness was just plain shittier than prior losses of love. All of these emotions made it doubly important for me to make it back to Athens for my birthday, the comfort of friends, and the warm confines of the country, familiar and reassuring.

Bloomington to Athens ain't that long a drive, so we left early in the morning and my anticipation for a party that evening heightened with each mile. I needed personal confirmation and friends, presents, and a party for elixir. For the whole trip I basked in the knowledge that the party plans had been left in good hands, the date was certainly set, and a crowd of well-wishers would greet me upon return to The Country Place.

With unbelievable excitement, and a being full of need, we drove the van up to the house. Except for a Cranfield greeting and the squawking geese, nobody was around. I desperately entered the house and not even a roomie was around. I called Cathy and Joe, only to be told casually that they did not know exactly when I would be home and so no party was imminent. I began to cry, which evolved into out-of-breath convulsing, sobbing in real pain, and silly self pity. Thankfully, Abby played it with a Zen philosophy of care and sympathy. She understood the reality of my expectations getting out of control and my needs becoming out of balance, all the while comforting me with her hand on my back as I lay there pathetically sobbing. As with most hurts, one recovers. She drove back to Athens and her apartment, and I had the country, a dog, two cats, a few geese, a bunch of chickens, thousands of fireflies, and the garden, all to myself.

The next evening, the party planners did their thing. Bowls of food, cases of beer, and some finely-rolled joints magically appeared as friends from near and far made the pilgrimage to the country for a proper celebration of my birthday. All was right with the world. But I had changed. No amount of studying, comp taking, or class discussion in all the interpersonal communication topics that had consumed me for years rivaled the learning of that trip with Abby. If justice should roll down like water and bless the blacks, if ethnocentrism should have no place in our international understanding of others, if those in poverty should be economically empowered, if those with disabilities should have every right to make smart and stupid decisions like the rest of us, and if by God they are going to let women vote, the least I could do was understand that being a "Southern Gentleman" could mean racism as well as sexism. After the party I read, with new interest and fascination, the book that Abby gave me for my birthday and left by my bed: Germaine Greer's *The Female Eunuch*.

Chapter 20: Magic Mushrooms
and Flying Feathers

On and off since comps, Bob, a few other Varmits, and I took care of the essential activities to conduct a top notch softball tourney in SE Ohio. We set the date, secured the two Athens softball diamonds on the Hocking with a small fee, and acquired the list of softball team names and addresses from local surrounds. Now into late July with time running out, we needed umpires, trophies, material to prepare the diamonds, and what seemed like a thousand other details.

"Scoop, we need a cart or trailer to sell some food and candy from," Bob said to me one day. "You know, a hot dog stand, with drinks, popcorn, candy, and other shit like that so we can make some money."

"OK, you got any notion of where to get such a thing?" I asked.

"Nope, but you can figure it out. I think maybe we can rent one in Athens."

With a few phones calls and some inquires with the Parks and Recreation Department, I obtained the rental rights to a very cool food trailer, replete with a fold-up door opening up a serving area and doubling as a shade awning. It also housed a cooler, a hotdog cooker, a popcorn machine, and a pop dispenser. The Varmits were going into business. The Lady Varmits, particularly French Fry, took over the cooking and serving, after I had figured out what to order in the form of food stuff. Fifty bags of buns, eighty pounds of hot dogs, thirty tanks of soft drinks, hundreds of bags of ice, dozens of boxes of candy, a fifty-pound sack of popcorn, twenty gallons of oil, and big boxes of cups, paper plates, plastic utensils, and other essentials.

The Varmits umpired the bases, while certified ones manned the plate. The fans were demonstrative when questioning a Varmit call at the bases, sometimes hurling drinks and wadded up hot dog holders. The Baron's Mens team, the hot team of that time locally, won the tournament. In spite of the rowdy exceptions, most fans had a good time and commented on the event being well-organized. That, however, would be the first and last softball tournament the Varmits would sponsor.

Meanwhile, back at the farm, our second garden far exceeded our first efforts. This time, I knew an ol' local farmer with a tractor and he plowed using a disc on the garden plot to ready the land by the machine designed to do so. Sure beat the hell out of a shovel in my blistered hands. We learned from experience, tons of zucchini did not overtake the farm, the corn seemed sweeter and the tomatoes grew bigger and juicier. But in the heart of the harvest season, my full-time country living came to a halt. After fifteen months at The Country Place, I moved back into Athens, to the South Green nonetheless, and assumed my place in a little one-bedroom apartment usually reserved for dorm counselors, but for me acquired through some wrangling with the graduate dean as a perk for serving as President of the Graduate Student Council. As you entered the dining room, a small open kitchen was the go-between into a bedroom, complete with a double bed, a real closet, and a bath, functional and unpretentious. That fall, I began having painful back problems, so the chores of the country were only romantically missed, for physically it would have been almost impossible.

Early in the semester, Mike was again visiting from Washington, DC, and, for nostalgia, we planned an adventure back to Meigs County to watch the Varmits in action. Rick, Ethel, Mike, Palmer, and I piled into the old maroon Chevy and headed west, with a stopover at Joe's house. Ethel was an undergraduate whom Rick had met in the Voight

Hall dorm where he lived in an apartment with Alice, his wife, who was a residential counselor. Ethel was crazy, a serious drinker/partier and fairly foul-mouthed, but fun to be around for entertainment purposes. Palmer was my new female love interest, since Abby moved to Bloomington and immersed herself as a serious graduate student. Palmer had authored numerous articles in the field of speech, hearing, and audiology. Like me, she was working on her dissertation. Palmer often bragged about being able to drink any man under the table; she loved adventure and a good time. Small, compact, and a world-class skier from Maine, she personified the independent spirit of Down Easterners.

Joe had the remaining stash of magic mushrooms. Each of us took a spoonful, gagged it down, and commenced to start a trip to a farm in Meigs County and a trip into the cosmos in our brains. Within the half hour drive south of The Country Place, the mushrooms began their journey through our bodies. Stories abound of other cultures in other places where servants of mushroom takers would save the urine released after their masters' trips, secured from their night pan, and upon drinking it, experienced the effects all over again. I never confirmed this factoid, but it is powerful testament to the reputation of the hallucinogenic. Finding farms in Meigs County is difficult under normal circumstances, and it was damn near impossible with four rowdy riders of the purple sage giggling like a group of school girls when a classmate passed a big stinky fart. My passengers had no idea where we were and I had not much more, but somehow we found a whole bunch of cars parked suspiciously by a farmhouse, and saw lights in a barn. We surmised that this must be the place.

"Shrooms," as they are affectionately known, possessed us. The laughing gas of nature, born of cow shit in the pastures of the world, a 1%

solution that puts the brain on alert, makes statues of hyperactive people who ingest, and can make your head melt while a five-mile smile seems permanently painted on your face. Petite, pretty, penis plants of innocence, yet brain wave stimulant of sophistication. Psilocybin, magic mushrooms, Liberty Cap, mushies, psillys, pixie caps, Welsh friends, Welsh tea, a tiny cap similar to the Phrygian bonnets adorning French revolutionaries storming the Bastille. Resembling the archetypal goblin's cap, appearing on T-shirts, posters and album covers in the late twentieth century, a five-hour trip to untamed lands, virgin mindscapes, and heightened awareness and focus bordering on manic and exhilarating. They will gag you, giggle you, and color your experience with ghastly light shows of planetarium proportions. Phallic undergrowth of pasture patties, ambrosia to the brain, transformed from meadow muffins to mind meanderings, Nureyev to the nervous system, hallucinogenic fungus created by the gods to inspire shamans, hippies, psychologists, researchers, poets, artists, and those brave enough to make a shake in the blender with a tablespoon of magic. Ingested, the small details, a bug, a swoosh of hair, a blade of grass, a shoe, can become quite beautiful and laden with meaning, revealing secrets unbeknownst before. But close your eyes and a full screen of cinematic wonder appears with colors oozing on a finger painting canvas of color, patterns and visuals, tints and textures, all on the eyelids of your theatre with matching soundtrack.

"Is this someone's farm?" Mike asked.

Now let me get this right. We had just come twenty miles from the nearest town through fields of corn and cows, to a place with a barn, a couple of tractors resting off to the side, an old combine, a grain storage bin, and fields as far as available light would allow us to see, and he asks that question.

"No, this is the government's space lab, where they keep the aliens," I mocked.

The trippers got hysterical, unable to control their laughter, so we sat in the car for a period of time (How long? Don't even ask, time is relative on mushrooms) to make sure that we did not enter the barn as laughing hyenas, tears streaming down our faces, and inappropriately irreverent to what was before us. Collected, and reassuring Mike that this was indeed someone's farm, we headed to the light of the barn and entered a door partially propped open. There sat a woman, an old farm lady I assumed, with few teeth left in her mouth. She had a tackle box full of money on the desk in front of her and she stared at us with eyes that said, "What the hell are you young city slickers doing at a cock fight?"

165

"I'm a Varmit and live over in Copperhead Hollow. How much does a ticket cost?"

"It's five bucks each," she replied, seemingly relaxing to our presence knowing that I was a local. Paying up, I noticed that the foyer of the barn contained a concession stand replete with hot dogs, popcorn, candy bars, and drinks. This was way too much stimuli for five higher-than-a-kite friends trying to fit into the scene and not do something stupid. So we proceeded to the fighting arena in the center of the building. We encountered barn-wood bleachers on four sides, about five rows deep, surrounding a small dirt pit with a three-foot wood wall. This was the fighting rooster's gladiatorial field of battle. In the corners between the bleachers the handlers were readying their cocks for their next entry. The birds were beautiful: red and yellow, and brown and black, and golden and silver with full plumes of feathers. Razor-sharp spurs, actually hooks, were strapped to their feet. As our entourage moved to an open space in the bleachers, I felt some security in sitting in one spot, a passive spectator to those around me, while my mind raced with images, imaginations, visuals, and stimuli. I had no earthly idea when they might appear or from whence they came. Smalley spotted me and pointed, and I could see him mouth, "Scoop." I tipped my hat to him and he returned to prepping his bird. The public address system announced the next two entries, and an older farmer in overalls and younger one in jeans entered the arena.

"I'll take five on the yellow jacket," yelled a boy from across the way as he pointed at someone near us. I guess his bet was acknowledged for he sat down with a satisfied look on his face. It started a bidding war, with fifteen to twenty people pointing at each other, shouting, "I take ten on the red head." This went on for a few minutes while we sat, stoned silent, clueless as to how the system worked, how one paid or collected debts, what the protocol was, or how to interpret this chaos. I tried to look cool while clinging to the bleachers, my hands firmly gripping the wood boards at either side of my seat. The handlers would hold the birds about head high and thrust them at the opponent, riling them up good, pissing off each other, and making sure the bird knew whom to attack. It reminded me of a prize fight weigh-in, with the fighters fake sparring, starring each other down at close range while verbally taunting the other, trying to puff up in order to ruffle feathers, there, figuratively, here, literally.

Some bell or announcer's command started the fight. The handlers, at the signal, would throw the birds at each other, step out of the ring, and watch with glued interest. Pride and money rode on the outcome; how much of each I had no idea. This was not an event for the faint of heart. This was a fight to the death or, as I learned, near death. The roosters would rear up, wings suspending them in midair, leading with their feet and spurs a shining, and with feathers a flying, they would try to puncture the other bird's body. They wrestled on the ground, and the beak became the weapon of choice, with each bird pecking furiously at the other's head, trying to draw blood. Every so often, the referee would stop the fight, check out a bird, make a ruling, and let the fight continue. When the actual fight was over was undeterminable to a novice, and, like a bullfight in Mexico, the death of the creature is not the only sign. I learned that many an injured bird is nursed back to fight again, with stories of miracle revivals, long careers in the ring, and near-reverence for the birds of legends. The array of humanity sitting in the bleachers was simultaneously pointing their fingers around at others until an acknowledged bet reached agreement, screaming their support for their bird of choice, munching on hot dogs, sharing recent farm gossip, and generally behaving like they all had met at a county fair in the animal barn for a show. My mind tried to figure the age range. Dismissing babies in the arms of parents, the free-standing and betting crowd ranged in age from about eight to well into the nineties. In fact, some of the most active betters comprised the younger ranks.

Getting high on mushrooms does not suspend one's morals or the ethical considerations as to the nature of good and evil. With a college degree in philosophy hanging on my wall back home, I pondered in my hallucinating brain the ethical arguments about chicken killing, betting, illegal activities, and my personal participation in such. But my Varmit friends were here and I was curious about them, so I suspended judgment in a sociological manner, just being open to the experience. I concentrated on trying to figure out the rules of conduct, the machinery of betting, how the handlers behaved vis-a-vis their fighting cocks, and how so many people could be enjoying a Saturday night at the fights, illegal as it may be. I kept my personal judgments at bay.

Years later, I went to a bullfight in Mexico City. I loved the hot chile pumpkin seeds and the beer sold in the stands while the matador sparred with the bull. One stuck bull ran around the ring spurting blood like a fire hose on the first few rows as it circled close to the stands before tiring and ultimately dying. It was not a pretty event. Neither was a cockfight. Watching an angry, spurred attack animal peck the head off his adversary or seeing a wound hole bleed through the feathers covering the bird, the ground, and the hands of the handler when retrieved from combat, is not a pretty sight either. Killing chickens for food and watching them kill each other for the sport of humanity were quite different activities. I had killed chickens before, an important cog in the cycle of life and death that produces the food we eat. If I was going to eat chicken, lamb, pork, beef, or any meat, then I could not hide behind the neatly wrapped packages in a super-market, wrapped in cellophane with a little diaper to soak up the excess blood and goo to make it more palatable for shoppers. Someone else is doing your killing for you, and you ought to know what that means in the scheme of existence. But standing in judgment, being holier-than-thou, thinking one is better than another because of a superior moral stance, just gets in the way of being totally in the moment. Years later I toured a tequila factory and fighting cock farm in Mexico, where they staged a mock tourista sanitized fake fight. As the group of Americans stood watching quietly and in judgment, I thought back to what I had learned about real rooster death in a real arena. I already knew how I felt.

None of us bet, mainly because of the mystery of it all, so we left after a couple of hours, said good-bye to Smalley, and headed out into the cool of evening. All Palmer could talk about was needing to pee. I am sure there was a restroom or privy somewhere but none of us could find one, so she boldly faced up hill, pulled her jeans and panties down, squatted down with the Milky Way swooshing across the sky, and peed. Now that was a first for me. But if guys can do it because they have plumbing that hangs out conveniently, what's wrong with a woman shaking her dew on a farm in the middle of nowhere, too? Of course, it called for a rousing chorus of Jerry Jeff Walker's immortal song:

"Pissing in the wind, bet I'm goin' to lose my friends
Making the same mistakes, we swore we'd never make again
And we're pissin' in the wind, but it's blowing on all our friends
We goin' sit and grin and tell our grandchildren."

Later that fall I would go one final time to a cock fight, with Rich, the infamous Boobsie Twin, and a couple of other fellow graduate students. Although we were not high as I had been that first time, the experience was not appreciably dissimilar. The same toothless farm woman sold us tickets, the betting remained a mystery, the death was just as real, and the people still carried on like it was a county fair. My appetite for this kind of adventure was satiated.

168

Epilogue

My third year in Athens kept me in contact with the Varmits at a few parties and for some beer drinking at Harpo's Bar, but our times together became more distant. Dr. Dave moved into The Country Place and assumed the responsibility of Cranfield, the cats, the geese and chickens, the remains of the garden, and one giant turkey. We saw each other on campus but not much out at the farm. One particularly cold winter day I caught sight of his very recognizable figure, still in his Postman's over jacket, trudging across the Campus Green.

"Hey Dave," I hailed.

He spotted the sound of a familiar voice and headed my way. At a shorter distance I noted a worrisome look on his face.

"Why so the long face?" I asked.

"Scoop, I've been meaning to call you. Cranfield got to running with other dogs and killed some sheep. They shot all the dogs. Cranfield is gone. I buried him up on the hill past the pond where he liked to roam. He's got a real good view of The Country Place."

I stood in silence, questions flooding my brain already full of hurt and emotion. How could this happen? He was such a sweet and gentle dog. A tear appeared, I asked Dave about a few details, who owned the sheep, who else lost dogs, and other things that were just cover-up conversation to real pain. Cranfield had lived a full life, but I surmised better ways to go. My quasi namesake became a victim of the law of the farm.

Just after attending my last cock fight in fall, I had a meeting scheduled with the President of the University at what he called his University Council. As Grad Council President, I assumed a seat along with the undergraduate student body president, lots of deans, a few faculty folks, and some business-office types. We met monthly, and the topic of concern that day was the apathy of the student body concerning student government elections. I listened intently to the diatribes and solutions bantered about the room, each of which, in my opinion, would have spelled disaster if implemented. Finally I spoke up and asked how truly committed were they to ending student apathy. Oh, they all feigned seriousness.

"If the president came out and said we should do away with student government because he had no confidence in students doing anything worthwhile around the university except drinking beer and doodling each other, and he did not trust students to really be involved in matters of state, then I could guarantee a 70% turnout at the next election," I said.

Silence.

"We could not do that, that would have the president lie," one dean remarked with imperial sanctimony.

"Now Ted, I do not want to set up an adversarial relationship with students by accusing them of such things," the president cautioned.

And on and on the reasons against my suggestion went. I responded saying it really wasn't lying since all of them had just expressed exactly what I was recommending the president say, they just did not have the guts to make it public. I learned in psychology and communication classes of a theory called paradoxical injunction. This situation seemed perfect to enact its magic. A paradoxical injunction is intended to restructure the system, for example, by having a parent and child alienated from each other work together to try to figure out the therapist's unusual, even bizarre, therapeutic prescriptions. So in the next election, less than 50% voted and nullified the election. I served out my term on the Council and on South Green, and, upon the president's request, repeated my performance at graduation, reprising my three minutes of fame at the podium of power. I did change the speech slightly and left Ohio University there soon after. My only legacy of note, one I persistently dogged the dean about for the whole year, was instituting a Graduate Student Council scholarship for a deserving grad student each year, and it still aids students today.

A couple of years later, when I was settled in Oregon and working for the state, a conference in Chicago drew my professional attention. At the conference, I ran into Patti (not the TCU ex), a friend from Ohio University days. After drinking some beer and swapping some lies our last night of the conference, we were wide awake past midnight and as youth are known to do, got a wild hair up our butts and decided to move our already planned next-day trip to Athens up. So by 1:30 a.m. we were packed and loaded, checked out of the hotel, and driving her car to the rolling hills of the Hocking. Around eight that morning, we serendipitously ran into WW on Court Street, said a few hellos and exchange hugs, and agreed upon a plan to get together later in the day. At that very moment, a truckload of Varmits, all piled in the truck bed soaking in the rays of the early morning sun, already shirtless and tanned for it was so late in the spring spotted me and did a double take. They hollered "Scoop, Scoop!" Mike, the catcher, yelled out as the truck rolled down the street, "Waverly, 8:30 tomorrow."

Patti and WW asked what that could possibly mean. I cogitated for a moment, and replied, "Must be a softball tourney in Waverly tomorrow morning."

After some reunion partying that night, I got Lucien, a friend still at OU, to take me to Waverly the next morning. Sure enough, the Varmits had assembled to play a little softball. Bob gave me a big hug, we did some round robin hand-slapping with the familiars, and I shook hands with the new recruits just before our warm-ups.

"Anybody got a left-handed glove Scoop can borrow?" Bob asked.

One was tossed my way and off to first base I trotted. A new guy asked Bob how come he wasn't playing first base like he had for a couple of years, and Bob answered. "'Cause Scoop is here, and he's our first baseman," and left it at that to the puzzlement and irritation of the new guy. But after a few of my legendary scoops at first base, a couple of base hits, and the reaction and interaction of the Varmits with me, he settled into a quiet respect that helped ease any feeling of interloper and usurper.

It felt like old times. We won a couple of games and spent some nostalgic times at Varmit State Park skinny-dipping and smoking some weed. Little Joe told me about Red Buzzard dying the past year. He had thirty years underground in West Virginia coalmines under his belt, another couple of decades farming, and ended up in an oxygen tent in the local hospital. Dying sterile like that just did not set well with Red, so he took out the tubes, got dressed, and announced to the hospital doctor and staff he was going home to die. With his breathing labored and his days numbered, Red went about what he knew best, farming. He beat the odds, lived years longer than anyone had expected, and never succumbed to the black lung that ravaged his chest. No, not Red. He was out working the field one day and a tree fell on him and killed him. Red died with his boots on, doing what he liked, needed to do, was called to do, or didn't know what else to do. We should all be so lucky. That would be my swan song with the Meigs County Varmits and their softball team. I boldly resumed my future back in Oregon for the next few decades.

After the millennium and my retirement, Rick, of West Virginia farm fame and my garden muse, and I were doing some consulting in central Ohio and decided to take a little journey down memory lane by driving to Athens. I had neither heard from, nor communicated with, any Varmit for over twenty-five years. Rick and I looked up an old friend who was still doing some counseling in Athens, and I suggested that we head out to Meigs County to check out The Country Place. We crossed the railroad tracks in Carpenter and made the big turn heading out of town, expecting to see the big Catawba tree.

"I was sure it was just about here," I said, pointing over left of the road.

"Stop the car, Rick," I instructed.

Getting out and looking around, I stumbled onto a stump, cut off at ground level, and with grass and weeds beginning to take hold, I paced it off. One, two, three, almost four steps, at about three feet each, and I figured the stump to be about ten feet in diameter. Yep, that was a big, wise, old tree. Now it was a ghost. I mumbled about how I had missed her, or old boy, or it, or something. Rick wondered what the hell was going on. I stood at the stump with rotting roots underfoot that once spread as wide as the branches above. Talking to a tree might be crazy, but mourning it as a fallen friend was beyond that. It left an emptiness inside me: a longing for the special times when it was my friend and listened to me.

It was only a couple of miles up and down the gravel road to The Country Place. We pressed on. We crested the hill and off to the left was the big open sheep pasture, actually just above The Country Place by juxtaposition, but distant by road. It was the field where Cranfield met his maker. I pictured a pack of domestic and wild dogs running and chasing after sheep for fun. The sheep would run away until they reached the far fence and then, not in their best interest, turn and run back, only to be intercepted by yapping and playful dogs. The dogs would nip at the sheep playfully at first, and then as the taste of wool and subsequently blood stirred primeval yearnings, the dogs would go on the attack, laying to waste many a defenseless animal, scattered across the field strewn with hunks of wool, stains of blood, and massacred sheep laying cold and bloody and dead. I heard a rifle shot ring out in my head and saw Cranfield falling in that field in my mind.

"Let's check out Irv's place," I said.

172

Just a few hundred yards down the road, on the other side, was where Irv's cabin should have been. We got out of the car and walked around. I found remnants of the fence that once held the old donkey, but there were few other landmarks left. Down the hill I tried to point out Little Joe's place, but it was no longer there either. Taking a left we entered the drive to The Country Place and drove up to the spot of the old chicken coop.

A new pre-fabricated house stood just beyond that spot. Off to the left, where my house used to be, there remained only a part of the old fireplace chimney, some crumbling foundation, remnants of the root cellar, and the big old oak tree that survived the massive lightning strike. Grass and weeds reclaimed the rest of the property. Rick and I could not roust anyone at the new house, so we walked around the place across the garden into the footprint of my old house. We stood by the spot of the big stove, walked out the imaginary front door that Cranfield destroyed trying to escape the wrath of lightning and thunder. We hiked up the hill to the pond with cattails still abundant, and gazed back down the hill to the ruins that marked the site of my fifteen months in Meigs County. I thought of the stuff I had left in the attic: a box of clothes, an antique butter churn, a bat, a glove, and other trappings of that past life. It wasn't things I longed for; it was deeper. I pondered that the place, the people, the parties, the perspective of time that would never be again, except in my memory. Slowly and silently we walked down the hill, returned to the car, and drove off into another life.

Later I would learn the fate of all the places on the Ridge, as the Varmits called it. Fire laid waste to Irv's 150 year-old cabin, Little Joe's place, Red's place, the Hilltop, and a few other Varmit farmhouses. With a wood burning fireplace and stove, an oil burning heater in the kitchen, the wood-framed Country Place was no match for flames. Thales, the Greek philosopher, wrote that everything on earth is made up of four elements: earth, water, air, and fire. Fire may be preeminent, for earth is formed from fire, and the heat of the sun allows the other elements to thrive. Fire certainly had the last word at The Country Place.

Rick and I drove back through Carpenter and headed out west to Laura's Store. There it sat, even updated, a real thriving little commercial enterprise still. I grabbed an ice cream bar from the case, a practiced endeavor, and introduced myself to the clerk.

"Have you heard of any people around here that call themselves the Varmits?" I asked.

"Yea, I've heard of 'em, but I don't think I really know any of them," she said. "But I've only lived out here a short time."

"Could I put a little note on the bulletin board by the door?"

"Be my guest."

So I drug out a business card, she supplied a piece of note paper, and I wrote that I was working on a book and trying to connect with the Varmits from the mid-seventies and could they give me a call?

Weeks went by and I had forgotten pretty much about it when an email appeared on my computer from Pam, the local hydrologist, who saw my note and card in Laura's. She wrote:

Ted,

I stopped at the little corner store on 143 last weekend and the owner asks me if I knew anything about the "varmints (sic)." I just happened to be an old "varmette" and still stay in touch with many of the "survivors" of that era. It is my understanding that you are writing a book and wanted to gather info. A few of us were trying to remember who you were. Can you write me a little about yourself and how you knew the varmints? That would be helpful. Maybe I can help.

Now I got to thinking. Varmits were usually avoiding the law and not really wanting to be found. Why would they respond to a guy from Oregon named Coonfield? Hitting myself on the forehead to indicate being a doofus, I remembered that my card only had my real name. The Varmits only knew me as "Scoop."

Writing Pam back, I talked about where I lived, and about knowing Irv and Little Joe, Smalley, Bob and Minibaugh, French Fry, and the others. I described the softball games, talked about being a student at OU, and mentioned buying milk at the Hilltop. But the line that connected all things Meigs County was this one:

"I was known as "Scoop" for my ability to pick up bouncers at first base on the Varmit softball team."

"Why didn't you say your name was "Scoop" before now? Hell they all know who you are and would love to get together and shoot the shit." Pam emailed me back.

"Duh!" I thought.

In the summer of 2004, I did another sojourn to Athens and called Pam up to see how I might connect with some Varmits. She gave me Little Joe's number and said to give him a call. He lived only about ten miles from Athens. I rang up the number from a pay phone on the outskirts of Albany at a little side-of-the-road diner. A familiar voice answered "hello."

"Little Joe, this is Scoop."

"SCOOP, SCOOP, how the heck are you?" he asked.

We talked a little and reminisced a little, and then he invited me to come by and visit.

He lived about the same distance northeast of Athens that Carpenter was southwest. A good hour later, right on the main highway through Chesterhill, I found his house.

It was unmistakably Little Joe who answered the knock. We hugged. He still smelled the same—body odor, heavy dope, and country. A few less teeth, the same remnants of the slight Brooklyn accent, and a stained green shirt covering his paunch, he was all Joe. He played a lot of online Euchre, a card game of fame around those parts. Who knew how he earned a living, but he was eager to hear about my life in Oregon. I told him about the book idea, and, with a few caveats about how much I really planned to write about, he blessed the project as a good thing.

"I'd like to get a few Varmits together from the old softball team so that we can sit down and chat about our time back then," I said.

Little Joe was silent for a while. Then he agreed.

"Yea, we could do that, it's been a long time since our last convention, '78 I think, and I've got a lot of email addresses. We could put out the word and have some folks show up."

"Do you want to do it this summer?" I asked.

"No, how about mid October? Yea, fall is a good time."

It dawned on me that the crop would have been harvested by then and the responsibilities would be at bay, so October was set.

When the time for the reunion arrived, I flew into Cincinnati, my friend Barry picked me up, and we went to his home in Oxford, where he was serving as a visiting professor of business at the university. After a short visit, our road trip commenced on the picturesque Highway 50, winding all the way from Cincinnati to Athens. Just before we entered Meigs County, I told Barry to turn off on the road to Raccoon Creek and Varmit State Park. The bridge had been totally restored and opened to traffic, but the place was not like I remembered. The creek now flowed muddy and the trees stood leafless; the sensuality was muted, it was quiet now. Nature was readying for winter. Vinton County had opened the bridge to traffic. It's a double multiple Kingsport truss-style bridge, and Barry took pictures of me on those rafters, and I thought of Nancy undressing on the rock right below us. I thought of the clear stream and cathedral of overhanging trees. I felt the bubbly massage of the water cascading over the rocks, now just a muddy stream.

We found Route 143 across the highway and east a little and we wound our way to Carpenter. I told Barry about the note left at Laura's as we passed, I explained about my buddy the Catawba tree, and I regaled him with other stories as we drove the still-gravel road to the top of the Hill, Carpenter Hill, in fact. We took a right toward Dyesville instead of going down the hill to The Country Place; there on the right was a conference center, our lodging for the next few days. It was fall: chilly, moist, with sun breaks that made the hills sparkle and dance with energy and the remaining summer flowers shimmer stunningly; they must have known their glory was fleetingly short.

Barry had never been to The Country Place, so the next day, before the party, I conducted a little "Ted's Varmit roots" tour, now more descriptively, certainly with less emotion.

That eve, I put on everything warm that I could find in my suitcase, gave an extra sweater to Barry, for winter was nearing and the outdoor party would surely to be on the edge of cool and uncomfortable. Following directions, even good ones, in Meigs County is dicey; did I mention that? Somewhere to the south, we pulled around a bend and spotted a beautiful pasture with a sweet little lake nestled in the middle of a verdant field. That's when we saw it.

"Holy shit," I cried out.

"What the hell is that?" Barry echoed.

There, a few hundred feet away, stood a giant white tent of circus-like proportions. This thing was 100 feet long, held up by huge metal poles with guy wires and stakes anchoring the whole monstrosity around the edges. A stage covered one end of the "grande chapiteau." Chairs and tables filled the middle portion, and food was spread out at the back. A table held a commemorative cake with a big "V" and "Reunion 2004" written in blue icing on white frosting. There was plenty of drink, mostly beer, of course. Near the tent, outdoor BBQ grills cranked out smoke and mouthwatering aromas, rented porta-potties lined up neatly off to the side, and there were people everywhere. I lost count at 200.

I immediately worried about how I was going to do serious book interviews at such a grand event. After the initial hoots and hollers of "Scoop, Scoop, Scoop," and once I had a joint handed my way, it became obvious my plans needed to shift, if not take a quick nosedive. The best I could do would be to get addresses and emails, ask some questions and try to remember the answers. I had come prepared with a small tape recorder, but this was a party, a reunion, a Varmit Convention. Serious literary research must wait for another context.

The gang was there: Irv, Lou, Paul, Bob, Chilly (Bob's brother and adjunct Varmit), Pam, Little Joe, Delia, Chugi, Tweeter, Smalley, Lou, and a host of others whom I did not know. Some wore Varmit Convention T-shirts from 1978; others sported the newer versions of their famous T-shirt "Varmit Entry" with a blurry red-eyed fighting cock smoking a big doobie. The faces had grown older and the mid-sections rounder, but the spirit of each Varmit still manifested itself in conversation, in what was said and unsaid. The years somehow did not distract from nor diminish the bond of brotherhood and friendship among the old softball teammates and their band of supporters.

Irv was clean-shaven and married with kids. He had made a little money selling dirt and, as always, delightfully and charmingly, was willing to talk about himself. I told him about Alice, Rick's wife, and how she used to get a wild look in her eye and say, "Irv, he's such a hunk!" Paul lived in Atlanta and was fighting cancer. Tweeter, in and out of mental hospitals for years, had finally acquiesced to the judge's request to either go to jail or get in school. He finished his education and became head of information systems and patient data in a hospital. His brother Lou matured into a solid citizen as well. Smalley married French Fry and ran restaurants in northern Ohio. His battery never ran down; he still talked a mile a minute and was as charming as ever. Bob and his brother stood cooking at the grill. Chilly was an EMT in his hometown. Bob hooked up with Darlene and they still lived in Athens County, near the Meigs County line. Harry wasn't there. Harry had spent some time in prison and now lived in a rundown trailer not far from the party. Someone said Harry became a skinhead or at least openly anti-Semitic. Mike, the catcher, not present either, captained an oil rig supply boat in the Gulf.

After I had shared a few stories with these old and dear friends, a guy approached me and I knew exactly who he was. I greeted him with, "Chipper, how the heck are you?"

"Just fine, Scoop, how's my favorite first baseman?" he replied.

We chatted, and he produced from his jacket pocket an old newspaper clipping and handed it to me.

"I just want you to have this as proof for your book that some stories are true."

It was the sports section of the *Spokane Daily Chronicle*, from July 5, 1973. Sure enough, there in the box scores in the line-up of the Spokane Indians, were Chip's stats.

The headlines, "Huge Throng Inspires Tribe" brought my eye to the article underneath.

"Inspired by the seventh-largest crowd to view Pacific Coast League baseball in fifteen years at the Fairgrounds, a Fourth of July gathering of 9388, the Indians sparkled at the plate and afield in registering a 7-4 triumph over Hawaii's Islanders."

The Indians were, in fact, a farm team of the Texas Rangers, a AAA team that was the last stop in the minors before being called up to play with the big boys.

The article continued: "Two run singles by Chip Maxwell, the young third baseman who also sparkled afield for the third straight night . . ."

His box score line read: "Mxwll ss 4,1,2,2" (abbreviated name, short stop, at bats, runs scored, hits, runs batted in).

Below in the box score, the article explained Chip hitting a double, so the sports writer didn't know what position Chip played or whether one of his hits was a single or double. Will Rogers, who only knew what he read in the paper, just rolled over in his Oklahoma grave. The Spokane Indians won back-to-back pennants in 1973 and '74, and a teammate of Chip's, a guy by the name of Bill "Mad Dog" Madlock, went on to be four-time Major League batting champion.

I smoked more good Meigs County weed that night than I had smoked in twenty-five years. The Varmit Band (of course they have their own band, hell, they have a State Park, remember?) cranked up the music. I danced with the pretty young fiancé of a Varmit kid, who, now in his twenties, drank beer and generally partied hardy. We played some Corn Toss or Corn Hole games with beanbags being tossed from thirty or so feet into holes in a clown's face. Late in the evening I had intimate conversations with my dance partner when she brought up the subject of having sex with two guys, and I gave fatherly advice, I think. Barry was nowhere to be found. We took pictures of everyone.

In one conversation, I found out how the Varmits got their name, a story I was not privy to until then. One summer, a group from Meigs

County (Smalley, Michael, Victor, Ivan, Kenny, and Donna), entered a volleyball tourney while traveling in Aspen, Colorado. When the sponsors asked for the name of their team, Smalley, or someone, said: "just call us the Meigs County Varmits." It was written down on the entry sheet V-A-R-M-I-T-S. Thus was born the name and its unique spelling.

Some of the guys asked me worrisomely how much I was going to write about certain Varmit activities in the book. Others were lobbying for being central characters. Most were supportive. Delia came up to me and with a serious look on her face asked, "Scoop, I know you are going to write about the Varmit softball team, but are you going to write about the Varmits being sexist?" After a slight pause, I responded, "I hadn't really thought about that. Tell me your perspective on it."

With little residual resentment and no misandry, but still fresh memories, Delia recounted stories of how she was treated as a woman, wife of a Varmit, and mother of a child. That's when I learned the reason for the lock on the refrigerator in her kitchen. In the midst of her struggling to make ends meet and provide food for her family, the cavalier Varmits would raid her fridge and ravish its contents, so she slapped a lock on it. I asked her to email me her experiences, for I could not by memory or by gender provide that perspective in my life with the Varmits.

A few weeks later the following arrived by email.

> Dear Scoop,
>   I think I should start by telling you that I feel the experience of having lived in Meigs County, 1970-1979, was one of the strongest events that helped to shape my life.
>   The reason I want you to know this is because I realize your book is about the Varmit ball team. To those of us that were seeking freedom, camaraderie, and had a need to learn the skills to live off of and be in touch with the land, Meigs Co. and the hurdles and joys presented was our school. The Varmit baseball team began as an outlet for all the macho-young men with ball playing skills. It served as entertainment for the rest of us. It was only a small portion of the experience for many of us.
>   The (Varmit) women that lived in Meigs. Co. were not considered equal to the men. It may have been that

*way everywhere in the U.S. at that time. We worked
alongside the men, partied with them, experienced the
same ups and downs of daily life but the masculine
species felt superior. This having been said, the
women that survived the experience are very strong
women that are well skilled and have vast survival
knowledge.*

*Chiriga Nina (Chugi) was born in Meigs Co. in
1974 in the house near the Dustbowl. She has always
been a very charismatic, bright individual. As a baby
she seemed to like to eat dirt. To her Dad, Mike,
and I, it just seemed like something she needed.
We lived for free in the house by the dust bowl,
where we had a milk cow, 2 pigs and 2 to 3 dogs. We
planted and harvested 5 acres of corn by hand to feed
the pigs and the cultivating was done by the
generosity of the neighbors.*

*We seldom had a TV or a radio and didn't have a phone.
We had a terrible time keeping a car running. Once
when Michael and I were on our way to a Varmit
ballgame in Athens, we only had enough gas to make it
to Laura's grocery in the car. We then parked the car
and hitchhiked to Athens, about a mile from the
ball fields we were still trying to get a ride when
here comes our car. The other members of the ball
team "hot wired" the car when they saw it at Laura's,
put some gas in it and waved and smiled as they passed
us by.*

*In about 1976, Michael and I bought 60 acres and an
old worn-out house on a hilltop half way between
Carpenter and Dyesville. No other house was visible
from the house of this property. It had a 1/4 mile
driveway and you had to park near the road and walk
to the house when it was muddy. Many times, we all
had to help carry groceries or laundry down the road
and Chugi always had to help as well. We had to
strain leaches out of the water from the well to use
it. For a while, Marlene the cow used to live on the
front porch and seemed to enjoy watching Green Acres*

on TV through the window. We had a chicken that used
to walk through the house and peck at crumbs on the
floor. I thought she was helping me clean.
This place was very secluded and usually a joy.
However Michael and I both having strong personalities,
and never able to compromise an argument,
helped to spin Chugi and I to the safety of my
parents house in Athens.

   Chugi was able to do well in school. She made friends
easily and has always had a good since of humor and a
keen grasp of what is really important in life. She
seems to have inherited good math skills from her
father and now is using them by working for a tax preparation
firm in Tennessee, where she lives with her husband
Frank and 3 children.

Delia

I read this over and over. Of course she was right, but I had never put two and two together and seen this from a woman's point of view. Sexism, racism, ageism, creationism, anti-Semitism, nationalism, and homophobia are diseases of either ignorance and/or flawed heritage. Like a recovering alcoholic, we must work each day to ensure we live in the health of tolerance. The Varmits did not teach me about sexism, but during my time in Meigs County I did realize that I must become a recovering sexist, shelving the vestiges of a southern gentleman upbringing, and facing the demon of prejudice each day.

My little gathering of a few softball players morphed into a certified Varmit Convention. Most of the team was there along with dozens of others. My notion of conducting a few calm interviews with old Varmits clearly was not going to work in the festive environment that prevailed. So I just jumped into the moment and re-experienced the expressions, language, and stories the same way that I had experienced Meigs County the first time around, some three decades before: with laughter, stories, lots of "butt, butt, buddies," reefer, beer, food, dancing, and friendship. If I was going to write a book, the specific details would have to come from the files of data in my own memory (a scary thought).

When the party wound down, I found Barry passed out on the front seat of a truck. I rousted him awake and drove him back to our lodging, over the hills and hollers of Meigs County, a skill honed so many times in bygone years. Passing The Country Place with the stars above, I felt all the warm feelings that good beer, dope, dancing, and a reunion of good people can provide.

A few years later I would again fly into Cincinnati, and my friend Charlie and I would drive over to Athens for a visit. Charlie had been one of my corporate consulting clients, and he had spent some time at OU teaching. This was a great opportunity for us to reconnect again with our past. I also needed to make a visit to show my respect to Beth, the widow of Little Joe, who had passed away a few weeks earlier. Bob invited us to a football pregame tailgate party, and Irv, Smalley, and a few spouses showed up. We all went to watch the Bobcats win one, a rare event I came to understand, and hung out after the game at a new chicken wing place into the evening. Charlie and I spent some time in a Court Street bar and got pretty wasted drinking Jameson's whiskey. We recounted Varmit stories to a group of young, naïve, very pretty sorority sisters. Luckily Charlie drove us back to the convention center on Carpenter Hill. The next day I showed him The Country Place, but by now I was accustomed to what it had become. We did find in the weeds the old pump that provided us water in the kitchen, now rusted and worthless, ah, but, priceless to me.

"Charlie, we're going to take this pump back to your house and one of these days you can mail it to me in Oregon. Good idea, huh?" I said.

Like a good sport he was willing to go along, so we snuck that old pump back to his car and stuffed it in the trunk. Sure enough, a few months later, a big, heavy box showed up on my doorstep, for the pump had made it home. We had breakfast at Bob and Darlene's house, and Bob welcomed us with cries of "Scoop and Harley." Not being able to hear very well at the ballgame when introductions happened, Charlie became "Harley" and the Varmits had struck again with a serendipitous and appropriate nickname. Harley only shook his head when he heard it. He knew that there was nothing he could do, so he became Harley forever to the Varmits.

I took more notes this trip, recorded road names and numbers, jotted down stories, listed the buildings in Carpenter, and sat quietly, and outlined this book, while Harley made some work calls. It has been in my head for thirty-plus years. My friend the tree is gone, the softball team is dissolved, The Country Place is in ashes, the Dust Bowl is pasture again, Cranfield's grave is unmarked, the cats, geese, and turkeys have long since vanished, three friends have fallen silent, and the Varmits have scattered.

On a cold November day, from the hill that defines Copperhead Hollow on the northwest, almost in sight of The Country Place, the ghosts of my time in Meigs County becomes my muse. Now, the story of my fifteen months living with Appalachian outlaws has been told. All that remains are the myriad other stories still nestled in those hills that need to be told as well.

The End

Acknowledgements

While writing this book, I needed frequent computer help from my friend Mike Ponder. While he was trying to explain the idiosyncrasies of my computer, my wife also chipped in some really good suggestions. But they noticed my still puzzled and bewildered look and joked, "It takes a village to raise an idiot." It might be true with this book as well.

My first debt extends to Dr. Bradley R. Rice, a retired college history professor, administrator, and senior editor of the journal of the Atlanta Historical Society for fifteen years, who just happens to be my friend of 44 years starting when we were freshmen roommates at TCU. Soon after he volunteered to take the first pass at editing these stories, his wife Vivian died of cancer unexpectedly. She would have loved this book, and I can see her shaking her head and saying something like: "Teddy John, did you really do that?" I miss her much. But Brad had me send him a hard copy of the text and between trips to Nepal and Oklahoma he dutifully worked his magic with my prose. He mailed me back sections of edited text. When I first looked at his "corrections," my heart sank. There was extensive editing on every page. "Could I be that bad of writer?" I thought. But I took a deep breath, launched into incorporating his edits, and accepted almost all of his suggestions. It was yeoman's work. Brad, you are a genius, a sweet man, and I am honored to have you as a dear friend.

In May of 2010, I met a young woman at my stepson's graduation party in a park in New York City. We chatted about life and she told me she was an editor. I, in turn, told her about my book in progress. I asked her if she knew anyone who could do a special kind of editing the publisher required of manuscripts. She said that's what she does. To trust my intuition and contract with Leslie Hendrickson to take the second swipe at editing this manuscript was, without a doubt, the smartest decision I made. She corrected the manuscript with such precision and detail that I marveled with each page at her unbelievable talent.

My wife, Meg Nightingale, read the manuscript as well and as a third editor found stuff all of us had missed. It was not an easy read for her, with way more detail of my escapades than she really wanted to know. But to her credit and as a gift of love, she has supported me throughout the creation of this project, and I am blessed every day to have her in my life.

My appreciation to other proofreaders, Suzy Soule fine-tuned lots of punctuation and grammar, and Maxfield Fulton, who found hundreds of needed corrections all of us had missed.

He is a genius with the English language.

My neighbor and friend, Bruce Rodgers, who admired the 70s style artwork as soon as I showed him the Varmit Entry T-shirt; his encouragement and help as a world-class graphic artist has been magical. For his talent and friendship I am grateful.

To the Varmits: this book is for all of you. Bob, the Varmit, without your help and support I could not have completed this project. Thanks to you and Darlene for all the Meigs County hospitality you provided on several occasions, driving me around the hills of southeast Ohio, and sharing the bounty of your garden, your stories, some pictures, and that twinkle in your eyes. It was truly entertaining just hanging around the farm and listening to you and Darlene squabble with each other. I love your sense of self, your candor, and your humor. You have always shared non-begrudgingly your life as an "outlaw." Irv, Lou, Paul, Hal, Beth, Delia, Smalley, Chip, Chilly, and Ed, and other Varmits that I knew in the past and met more recently, all of you have contributed by being yourselves, sharing stories, and trusting me enough to write about our time together.

To my friends and golf buddies, Rick Nida, Jon Helser, Dave Kvamme, Barry Spiker, Mike Ponder, Charlie Slaven, Ron Faunce, Merlin Whitmore, Joe Chilberg, Diane Garga, and Bob Fischbach: thanks for listening to my pain and excitement for so many years while creating this book. Flash, you were my muse. So many times when I finished a section, and as I reread it, I'd hear your laugh and know that there would be at least one solidly appreciative reader. You kept me writing. Barry, your support, your gifts of books, videos, and loving nagging kept me focused as well. Thanks for taking me to the Varmit 2004 Reunion and becoming an honorary Varmit. Charlie, you, in turn, sojourned with me to Meigs County and kept an open mind about another culture in Ohio quite different from your life in Cincinnati. My thanks to Diane Slaven, the best Midwest cook I know, whose hospitality and companionship on road trips made my visits so much fun. My thanks to my dear friend, Rick Nitti, who more than anyone else, so graciously listened to my daily reports of the victories and vicissitudes associated throughout all the years this project was in process. David Hunt, thanks for the pictures and all the good times. And finally, I will miss so despairingly being able to give a copy of this book to Dianna Ponder and Dave; both have left a giant hole in my heart.

Finally, thanks Bit-O-Honey; you're the best.

Cover Art Credit

Lad Jeric, now deceased, created the original fighting cock art work in the early seventies for a T-shirt that read "Varmit Entry." The adaptation for the book cover and lettering is by Bruce Rodgers, a graphic artist in Portland, Oregon.

bruce@brucerodgersdesign.com

Permissions and Credits

Grateful acknowledgment is made for permission to reprint song lyrics from the following copyrighted works:

1) "Strike a Match and Light Another" by Jay Ungar
   Alfred Music Publishing, 1970. Used by permission.
2) "I heard You Been Laying My Old Lady" words and music by Rusty Weir
   Used by permission of Crossfire Productions, Inc.
3) "Pissin' in the Wind" words and music by Jerry Jeff Walker
   Used by permission of Groper Music, Inc.
4) "Athens County"
   Written by Jonathan Edwards and Joseph Dolce
   © 1971 (Renewed 1999) CASTLE HILL PUBLISHING LTD. (ASCAP)
   Administered by BUG MUSIC
   All rights reserved. Used by permission
   Reprinted by permission of Hal Leonard Corporation
5) "Going to the Country"
   Words and Music by Steve Miller and Ben Sidran
   Copyright © 1970 by Sailor Music
   Copyright renewed
   All rights reserved. Used by permission.
   Reprinted by permission of Hal Leonard Corporation
6) "Baby I'm a Want You" © 1972 Sony/ATV Music Publishing LLC.
   All rights administered by Sony/ATV Music Publishing LLC., 8 Music Square West,
   Nashville, TN 37203. All rights reserved. Used by permission.
7) "Make it with You" © 1970 Sony/ATV Music Publishing LLC. All rights administered by Sony? ATV Music Publishing LLC, 8 Music Square West, Nashville, TN 37203.
   All rights reserved. Used by permission.

Songs by the Grateful Dead, Copyright© Ice Nine Publishing Company
   "Eyes of the World" lyrics by Robert Hunter
   "Ithica" lyrics and music by Robert Hunter

"The Only Time Is Now" lyrics by Jerry Garcia, music by the Grateful Dead

"Feel Like a Stranger" lyrics by John Barlow, music by Robert Weir

"Sugar Magnolia/Sunshine Daydream" Lyrics by Robert Hunter and Robert Weir, music by Robert Weir

"Uncle John's Band" lyrics by Robert Hunter, music by Jerry Garcia

"Weather Report Suite, Part I" lyrics by Eric Anderson and Robert Weir, music by Robert Weir

"You Remind Me" lyrics by Robert Hunter, music by Mickey Hart and Warren Haynes

"Truckin" lyrics by Robert Hunter, music by Jerry Garcia, Phil Lesh, and Robert Weir

Soon after I sent a letter to Ice Nine Publishing Company, the owner of all the Grateful Dead intellectual property, I received a call from Alan Trist, their Chief Operating Officer. He spoke with an endearing British accent and wanted to ask me a few questions about my book. He was concerned about the lyrics being used exclusively around drug use and I reassured him that they were not, although I told him this was a book about the 70s and, in fact, drugs were a part of what we did back then. As an example, I told him about the context of "Sugar Magnolia" and he began to sing along with me on the phone.

"Oh, I was there, and I understand," he said. We had a delightful conversation and I learned he had worked at Ice Nine since 1970. He gave me permission to use all the Grateful Dead song lyrics without a fee. Thanks Alan, you made my day!

CPSIA information can be obtained
at www.ICGtesting.com
Printed in the USA
FSOW01n0935250516
20786FS